JESUS OF ISRAEL

Jesus of Israel

FINDING CHRIST IN THE OLD TESTAMENT

Father Richard Veras

PUBLISHED BY ST. ANTHONY MESSENGER PRESS
CINCINNATI, OHIO

RESCRIPT

In accord with the *Code of Canon Law*, I hereby grant my permission to publish *Jesus of Israel: Finding Christ in the Old Testament* by Father Richard Veras.

Most Reverend Carl K. Moeddel
Vicar General and Auxiliary Bishop
of the Archdiocese of Cincinnati
Cincinnati, Ohio
November 7, 2006

Scripture passages have been taken from *New Revised Standard Version Bible,* copyright ©1989 by the Division of Christian Education of the National Council of the Churches of Christ in the U.S.A., and used by permission. All rights reserved. (Note: The editors of this volume have made minor changes in capitalization to some of the Scripture quotations herein. Please consult the original source for proper capitalization.)

Excerpts from the English translation of the *Catechism of the Catholic Church* for the United States of America, copyright ©1994, United States Catholic Conference, Inc.—Libreria Editrice Vaticana. English translation of the: *Catechism of the Catholic Church Modifications from the Editio Typica,* copyright ©1997, United States Catholic Conference, Inc.—Libreria Editrice Vaticana. Used with permission.

Cover design by Mark Sullivan
Cover illustration is a detail from the painting, *Ecce homo,* by Il Sodoma, also known as Giovanni Antonio Bazzi (1477-1549); Galleria Palatina, Palazzo Pitti, Florence Italy; Photo Credit: Nimatallah / Art Resource, NY
Book design by Phillips Robinette, O.F.M.

Library of Congress Cataloging-in-Publication Data

Veras, Richard.
 Jesus of Israel : finding Christ in the Old Testament / Richard Veras.
     p. cm.
 Includes bibliographical references and index.
 ISBN-13: 978-0-86716-772-6 (pbk. : alk. paper)
 ISBN-10: 0-86716-772-6 (pbk. : alk. paper) 1. Bible. O.T.—Criticism, inter-
pretation, etc. 2. Bible. N.T.—Relation to the Old Testament. 3. Jesus
Christ—Person and offices—Biblical teaching. 4. Jesus Christ—
Messiahship. I. Title.

BS1171.3.V47 2007
221.6'4—dc22

                          2006028792

ISBN 978-0-86716-772-6

Published by Servant Books, an imprint of
St. Anthony Messenger Press
28 W. Liberty St.
Cincinnati, OH 45202
www.AmericanCatholic.org

Printed in the United States of America.
Printed on acid-free paper.

07 08 09 10 11 5 4 3 2

For my parents, Laurence and Alicia,
who handed on to me their precious faith

Contents

Foreword

One of the greatest blessings of my life came the day I met a seminarian named Rich Veras in a homiletics class at St. Joseph's Seminary in Dunwoodie, New York, where I was teaching at the time. I was struck by Rich's wise demeanor, his exceptional preaching and his amazing certainty that belied his young years.

Since then Father Rich's priesthood has reached a remarkable and beautiful fruition. Readers of *Magnificat* are well acquainted with his regular essays, which many esteem to be their favorite part of the magazine. Moreover, Father Rich is a teacher, preacher, parish priest, recorded songwriter, theatrical director, chaplain to the young and now author of this, his first book.

Jesus of Israel helps to fulfill something that our Holy Father Pope Benedict XVI deems supremely important. In an interview that he gave in 1996, then Cardinal Joseph Ratzinger said,

> We must live and reflect on our relation to Judaism in a completely new way…. It has to be lived on the basis of reverence for one another and of an interior belonging together. We are on our way to that point. I think that the existence of the Old Testament as a part of the Christian Bible has always made for a deep inner affinity between Christianity and Judaism…. Our belonging together through the common history of Abraham,

which at the same time separates and brings us together, is something we have to live anew.[1]

The teaching of *Catechism of the Catholic Church* emphasizes this seminal truth:

> "The economy of the Old Testament was deliberately so oriented that it should prepare for and declare in prophecy the coming of Christ."… The books of the Old Testament bear witness to the whole divine pedagogy of God's saving love.… The Church…has illuminated the unity of the divine plan in the two Testaments through typology, which discerns in God's works of the Old Covenant prefigurations of what he accomplished in the fullness of time in the person of his incarnate Son. Christians therefore read the Old Testament in the light of Christ crucified and risen.… The New Testament has to be read in the light of the Old.… As an old saying put it, the New Testament lies hidden in the Old and the Old Testament is unveiled in the New. (*Catechism of the Catholic Church* [*CCC*], 122, 128, 129)[2]

With insight, intelligence, humor and pastoral passion, *Jesus of Israel* enables us to grasp and live anew this "deep inner affinity" so vital for the Church and our own personal happiness. One comes away from this book with a new appreciation of sacred Scripture and a new ability to recognize the traces of Jesus Christ in even minute circumstances of everyday life. This beautiful book generates in the reader a new fervor for the faith by demonstrating compellingly how "the Gospels are the heart of all the Scriptures" (*CCC*, 125).

Father Peter John Cameron, O.P.
Editor-in-Chief, *Magnificat*

Introduction:
The Long-Awaited Messiah,
the Promised of Ages

A number of years ago a Jewish man asked to speak with me at the end of a Rite of Christian Initiation of Adults (RCIA) session in the parish. Eric had been attending the sessions throughout the fall. Our last session before Christmas traced the history of the kings of Israel and highlighted the promise to David that his kingdom would last forever through one of his descendants. We always did this in Advent so that when our catechumens heard the name "David" repeated throughout the Advent and Christmas seasons, they would understand its significance and recognize that Jesus, a descendant of David, is the fulfillment of an age-old promise.

Eric had started coming to the RCIA because a recent tragedy in his life had convinced him that his family "needed religion." It didn't seem to matter to him which religion, but Catholicism seemed the obvious choice. His wife was a baptized Catholic, and since this "religion thing" was his idea, he couldn't expect her to go to Hebrew classes.

Until this particular evening Eric, while being very willing to read the materials and listen to my lectures, seemed rather uninvolved. He had kind of a "whatever you say, Father" attitude. But at the end of this meeting, he seemed to have something serious on his mind. He waited until everyone else had left before speaking to me.

As tears moistened his eyes, he said to me, "Father, no one ever told me he was from the line of David."

Eric was not from a strict Jewish family, but through the Hebrew education he had received, he knew that the Messiah was supposed to come from the house of David. Until he was shown that Jesus was indeed of the house of David, he thought that the Christian Messiah was just some charismatic leader who came on the scene, seemingly from nowhere. He thought Christianity was separate and disconnected from Judaism. He was willing to profess belief in Jesus only so his family could have some kind of generic religion and thus an equally generic connection to God.

On that evening, however, Eric discovered that Jesus had everything to do with the age-old longing of his people, a longing so strong and specific that it still echoed in the heart of a secularized man who had limited knowledge and practice of Judaism. From that evening on his curiosity about Jesus was real, so real that it strengthened him to make a number of sacrifices over the next few years that turned his curiosity into faith and love. On the day of his reception into the Church, he was not living a generic faith but a faith in the Person of Jesus Christ. It was a faith based on the experience of a personal God who works in history and is present today.

Monsignor Luigi Giussani, founder of the international Catholic movement Communion and Liberation, once wrote, "We can understand Christian experience only with difficulty if we are unwilling to relive the history of the people of Israel, in all its aspects and in all its drama."[1] For me Eric is a verification of that statement.

And what does this statement say about the understanding that "cradle Catholics" have of Jesus of Nazareth, the Messiah? Does the heart of the typical Catholic leap at the words that the angel Gabriel said to Mary, "The Lord God will give to him the throne of his ancestor David" (Luke 1:32)?

Do we wonder why the angels announced the birth of Jesus to shepherds? Why not carpenters? Why not rabbis?

Why is it so important that Jesus was born in Bethlehem, the city of David? Why will Jesus stop dead in his tracks when a blind man calls out, "Jesus, Son of David, have mercy on me" (Mark 10:47)?

The Importance of Memory

If we are not aware of the history of the Jewish people, then we are not as aware as we can be, as we are invited to be, of the mercy of God revealed in Jesus Christ. Jesus did not come from nowhere! He was long awaited by a people who were educated uniquely and mysteriously to expect God's presence in the messiness of their own history.

The Jews expected God to be with them, and when he seemed to be absent, where did they turn? They expected God to be victorious, and when he seemed to be defeated, where did they turn? They expected God to be merciful, and when he seemed not to be, where did they turn? It was memory that kept alive their expectation, their hope.

For the Jewish people memory is not a nostalgic recollection of the past but rather the recalling of an event that affects them in the present. It is not so much "remember the good old days" as it is a mother saying to her uppity child, "Remember who you're talking to." It is like the reprimand to a person speaking loudly in a church or library to "remember where you are." Memory is the recalling of a fact that resonates before me now.

After coming into the Promised Land, for instance, the Jewish people would offer God each year the first fruits of their harvest. When they brought those fruits to the priest, they had to recite a narrative recalling what God did to free them from slavery in Egypt and to bring them into their own land (see Deuteronomy 26:1–11). Their prayer expressed the fact that those fruits that they presented to God at that time were themselves the result of all God did to free them; these were fruits of the Promised Land he gave them. They were literally the fruits of God's saving action. Those offering the first fruits recognized them as a sign, in the present, of all that God had done to save them.

Jesus takes up this notion of memory when he tells his disciples at the Last Supper (the first Eucharist), "Do this in remembrance of me" (Luke 22:19). In the sacrifice of the Mass, the risen flesh of Jesus is really present because of all he did to save us. His incarnation, suffering, death and resurrection bear fruit that is present here and now.

For a Jew the greatest possible sin is to forget. Loss of faith and all other disloyalty result from forgetting the saving actions of God. The Old Testament is full of warnings against forgetfulness. If a Jew forgot all that God had done to bring him or her into the Promised Land, then the first fruits would seem like ordinary fruits, no different from the fruits harvested by pagan neighbors. After a while the Jew might forget to offer them or might offer them only as a formality, a rite not much different from the religious rites of the pagans. And if the religious rites of their pagan neighbors seemed more glamorous and attractive than theirs, it would be quite easy for a forgetful Jew to engage in what he would see as parallel practices.

If we do not understand and remember all that God did to prepare the Jewish people and the world (in that order!) for the coming of Jesus Christ, if we don't recognize Jesus as the fulfillment of this long history, then Jesus can seem to us like just another religious figure, not much different from others whose altruism and godliness have distinguished them. His claim of divinity can seem a bit outlandish. We can think of Christianity as "my religion" the way America is "my country" or my old high school or college is "my *alma mater*." We can see our devotion to Jesus as not much different from the devotion of those of other faiths. Our faith can become generic and our worship formalistic.

FAMILIARITY WITH JESUS

The purpose of this book is to inspire the wonder that Eric experienced when he discovered Jesus as the answer to the hope of his people, the unique fulfillment of a unique history. This wonder is the fruit of remembering the merciful and victorious presence of God as it has played out in an extremely dramatic history: a history full of betrayals and contradictions yet, in the end, gloriously and miraculously coherent—a fulfillment of human expectation that is beyond all imagination!

As happened with Eric, the wonder in front of Jesus should lead to familiarity and love. Continuing the Old Testament imagery of God as the faithful husband of his people (see Isaiah 54:5–6; 62:5; Hosea 2), the New Testament describes

Jesus as the Bridegroom of the Church (Matthew 9:15; Luke 5:34–35; John 3:29; Ephesians 5:25–33). Thus the long-awaited Messiah comes into the world to propose himself to us in marriage, to invite us into an intimate communion with him.

If you are in love with someone to the point of contemplating marriage, you want to know that person's history. You want to know the family that will become your own. Familiarity with your spouse's history helps you to know him or her better. It helps you understand the person's actions and words, gestures and phrases. The less you understand your spouse's history, the more he or she is a stranger to you. The more you know of your spouse's family and history, the greater your familiarity and unity.

The history of the Jewish people is the history of Jesus; to see it as something separate or irrelevant is a sad diminishment of Christianity. To see the God of the Old Testament as somehow not the same person as the merciful Father whom Jesus reveals is an ignorance or a forgetfulness that carries within it the seeds of doubt.

Instead of teaching RCIA, I now teach in a boys' high school, but the goal is the same: to educate and thus communicate certainty in Jesus Christ, present here and now. I do not teach or preach the Scriptures as something to be admired as ends in themselves. I teach so that through the Scriptures, and most especially through the Gospels, I can help my students know and recognize Jesus Christ, present here and now in his mystical body, the Church. For without the contemporary witness of the Church, the Gospels are mere texts.

More than anything else, I desire with this book to aid the reader to come to a deeper certainty about Jesus Christ. His certainty is what first struck those who encountered Jesus. Certainty is what characterizes those Christians today who can answer with a joyful and resounding yes Jesus' timeless question, "When the Son of Man comes, will he find faith on earth?" (Luke 18:8). May he find in the Church a living faith that is full of wonder because it is bursting with the memory of his presence.

CHAPTER ONE

What Makes the Chosen People Unique?

In the Old Testament God reveals that men and women are made in his image—not just Jewish and Christian men and women but all men and women, including those who lived before the call of Abraham and the genesis of the Jewish people. If I am in God's image, then there must be something in me that is infinite. What do I experience in myself as infinite?

Intelligence? Certainly not!

Patience? No!

Ability to love? I love my family and friends poorly, and I have great difficulty loving those who annoy me. (When someone drives too slowly in front of me in New York, I find myself driving right up against the limits of my ability to love.)

While I may learn more and acquire more patience and become more and more able to love right now, I don't experience these things as infinite. What is infinite in me right now? Desire!

Men and women never stop wanting. If we get what we want, very quickly we want more, or we want to improve what we have. This is nothing to be ashamed of; it is the very thing that makes us godlike. Our limitless desire is a mirror image of God's limitless being.

This infinite desire is coupled with severely limited abilities, so that we can never completely satisfy ourselves. Something in the very fabric of our being tells us that we are made for a complete satisfaction that we cannot define or explain or imagine. All music, poetry, literature, art and philosophy are somehow expressions of this tension between our infinite desire and the fact that everything else about us is limited.

Human religions express perhaps most directly this tension. Throughout history human beings have tried to reach beyond their limits to some kind of higher powers that can give meaning to their strange existence and perhaps can offer some kind of answer to their mysteriously infinite desire. This attempt to seek out a mystery beyond the limited world is natural and reasonable. It was common to all times and places until the occurrence of something uncommon, something unknown before, something truly new. Jews and Christians do not claim that we have found the mystery; rather, the Mystery has entered history. He has sought and found us.

God Meets Human Desire

God entered history definitively in Jesus Christ, the man from Nazareth who is God in the flesh! Jesus' first words to his first two disciples are "What do you seek?" (John 1:38). The Word made flesh addresses himself to human desire, which is the mirror image of the response—"the way, and the truth, and the life" (John 14:6)—that he is.

This encounter between two men and God was possible because God took the initiative to enter the world so that these men could bump into him. Jesus Christ is not the fruit of his disciples' ideas; he is a fact. Familiarity with Christ comes from knowledge of him, gained from time and life shared with this carpenter from Nazareth, this Son of God.

God's coming among us as a present fact in time and space is definitive in Jesus Christ, but to prepare for this coming God planted verifiable evidence of his pending entrance into history. If a couple is going to have a baby, you see all kinds of signs that herald the baby's coming: the changing shape of the mother, the painting of a room, the collection of all kinds of baby paraphernalia and, most interestingly, a change in the behavior and mentality of the young couple. In the same way we see signs of Christ's coming in his family history, the history of the Jewish people.

Two thousand years before Christ, God chose Abraham, and from Abraham grew a people whose behavior and mentality were very different from those of any people who came before them. The people into which Jesus would be born made (and still make) the audacious claim that they are the chosen people of God. Such a claim must be backed up by evidence. You would not allow a man claiming to be a police detective to enter and search your home if you did not first see a badge. We shouldn't believe the Jews' claim to be the chosen people if they cannot show us something to back this up. When we look closely, we see that their history is their badge.

THE JEWISH PEOPLE ARE EVIDENCE OF A GOD WHO MEETS US
When I teach my students about the unique attributes of the Jewish people, I begin by slamming my hand against the blackboard. I ask the students to imagine the janitor cleaning the school that night. When he comes into the classroom,

what will he know? He will know that someone put a hand-print on the blackboard. If someone tries to tell him that no one was in that classroom all day, he will not be convinced, because the handprint wasn't there the night before, and handprints don't just appear on blackboards.

After listening to my students recount plots of various horror movies that this image evokes, I invite them back to reality and explain that the Jewish people are like God's handprint on the world. Their history simply makes no sense if there is not Someone beyond the limits of this world who has chosen them.

BELIEF IN ONE PERSONAL GOD

The most obvious attribute of the Jewish people, which distinguished them from all peoples before them and around them, is their belief in one personal God.

As we have said, all peoples somehow reached out to powers beyond human limits and the limits of the world. Many assigned different forces of nature to different gods, so you get the polytheism of Egypt, Greece, Rome and peoples of the American continent. Other peoples ascribed different gods to different peoples and different localities. We also find imaginings and speculations of an impersonal force existing behind everything. But you can't talk to a force, and you can't have a relationship with a force. We don't negotiate with hurricanes, even if we do give them names.

The Jews are sons and daughters of Abraham, and they had a mysterious encounter with what was definitely not a force but a Person. Over time spent in a very dramatic dialogue with this Person, they came to believe that he is the only

God, the one true God. All other gods are false; they simply don't exist.

It is important to recognize the audacity and seeming absurdity of this claim when the chosen people first asserted it. Before great polytheistic cultures—which produced impressive architecture, theatre and systems of laws, not to mention hanging gardens—the Jews, a relatively powerless people with not much to show for themselves, stand with pride and certainty and say, "Your gods are fake; ours is the only real one!" Perhaps we see here the genesis of the Jewish sense of humor.

What is amazing is that this claim, which no previous people had thought of, corresponded so completely to the human heart. Today if you ask people if they believe in God, they know that you are asking if they believe in one personal God. If someone were to ask, "Do you believe in gods?" it would be very difficult to take the question seriously.

The monotheism of the Jewish people is extremely important in preparing them for the coming of Jesus Christ. Indeed, they were the only people capable of understanding Jesus' claim to be the Son of God and therefore God himself. Even those who would not believe in him were capable of being scandalized only because they understood that Jesus was claiming to be the source of everything, the one true God.

If Jesus had come to any other people, his claim could provoke neither faith nor rebellion because it would not be understood. If he had gone to the Greeks, they might have said, "Great, we'll worship you. Which of the gods is your father?" Recall that in Acts 14 the people in Lystra began to worship Paul as Hermes, because he talked a lot, and they worshiped Barnabas as Zeus.

Praying to the One True God

The Jewish people prayed to this one true God with an amazing lack of fear. Perhaps the most astounding of their prayers are the psalms of lament or complaint, and the most astounding among these would be those psalms in which they complain to God about God himself! Psalm 44, after a long list of all the things that God has not done for Israel in a difficult situation, exclaims,

> Rouse yourself! Why do you sleep, O Lord?
>> Awake, do not cast us off forever!
> Why do you hide your face?
>> Why do you forget our affliction and oppression?
> (Psalm 44:23–24)

The Jews are telling the one true God, "Don't just stand there; do something!" While other peoples are making human sacrifices to appease their gods or to get a good harvest, the Jews are yelling at theirs! They are complaining with no fear of retribution. Psalm 77, after recalling how great the Lord used to be, laments, "It is my grief / that the right hand of the Most High has changed" (Psalm 77:10). In other words, "I liked you better before."

These complaints are amazing when you consider how fearful other peoples were of their gods. In fact, you would think the Jews would be more fearful of their one God, since he has all the power to crush them if they cross him, and there are no other gods to which they can appeal if he gets angry. Instead the Jews pray to God with unparalleled confidence and familiarity. They are not afraid to be completely honest in front of the one and awesome God, evidenced by the fact that the psalms are filled with every kind of human emotion, from rejoicing and thanksgiving to near despair.

In fact, when the Jews pray to this one God, they seem to be treating him like a father. When children complain to their parents, are they afraid that they will be killed or kicked out of the house? No! And doesn't every parent wish that his or her children would be free to be completely themselves and totally open and communicative? This does happen in the relationship between Israel and God. This God seems to be the ideal father!

Jesus will come to the Jews precisely to reveal to them that God is their father, and not just their father but *the* Father, *our* Father. This is the definitive revelation of a relationship with God already begun. The familiarity and fearlessness with which the Jews relate to the one, all-powerful God is truly something beyond the limits of human hope or imagination. It is something from out of this world that entered this world.

GOD'S TIME

Until the call of Abraham and the generation of the Jewish people, all peoples saw time as cyclic. From this perspective, all of life goes around in the same circle, out of which you cannot break and from which you cannot move forward. We speak of people "thinking outside of the box." Well, before the Jewish people, it seems that no one was able to think or imagine their way out of this circle.

The cyclic view of time is understandable when you consider nature. Every day we see the cycle of the sun. Every year we see the seasonal and agricultural cycle. Every few years we see livestock born, live, give birth and die. The cycle of human life would have been much more apparent to the ancient peoples than it is to us. With shorter life spans and all generations living together, by the time someone was ten years old, he or she probably would have seen birth and death a number of times.

Life is full of cycles, and so time was seen as cyclic. The Chinese calendar, for instance, is on a sixty-year cycle. Perhaps this notion of time inspires beliefs in reincarnation and fate. If I can't go beyond the circle, yet I have this sense that there is something infinite about my life, then I imagine that I will reenter the circle and start all over again.

The Greeks had a strong notion of fate. If something was fated to happen to you at some point in your life, at some point in the circle, there was absolutely nothing you could do to escape it. Sophocles' *Oedipus Rex* is all about the inescapability of fate.

The Jewish people were the first to break out of this way of thinking, evidenced by the fact that they numbered their years, calculating from creation through their history. The numbering of years makes a claim that time does not repeat itself. Time is headed toward a destiny. This day of this month of this year will never come again; it is a moment on a road that has a goal.

How did the Jews come to have this notion of time? Perhaps because the God of Abraham kept making promises to the Jewish people that they themselves would not see but that their descendants would see. He promised Abraham descendants as numerous as the dust of the earth, but Abraham would not live to see them all. He told the Jews in the desert that their children would see the Promised Land. He told David that a king would come from his line whose kingdom would last forever. He promised the Jews that a Messiah would come. All these promises would be fulfilled in the future, and so the Jews would hope that their children would see what they did not. Jesus would tell his apostles that many prophets and kings had longed to see what they saw but did not (see Luke 10:24).

This notion of time as a road headed toward destiny also exalts human freedom. I am not trapped by fate. The decisions I make today will affect the future. Human action acquires new weight when it can echo into the unseen future and stretch toward eternity. This notion of time is thus another witness to man as the image of God.

In a cyclic view of life, why would you want more for your children? They simply are going to go through the same circle of life as you. Why would your decisions matter? The cycle is going to repeat itself regardless. Thank God for his choice and education of the Jewish people! Thank God that the circle is broken!

When Jesus enters the world and brings the Good News to all peoples, he extends to them the possibility of breaking out of the circle. For this reason it is appropriate that the Christian world numbers our years from the new creation, the coming of Christ.

The Unbroken Witness

The continued existence of the Jews as a people is miraculous when you think that from the fall of Jerusalem in AD 70 until 1948, they didn't even have their own land. They had been dispersed throughout the world for centuries yet had not forgotten that they belonged to this unique people who arose as one among the tribes of the Middle East desert four thousand years ago. They seemed no match for the great cultures among whom they wandered and under whom they lived, and yet they lived with a view of God and a view of the person and a view of history completely new and infinitely more adequate to the human person than anything proposed in any other religion or philosophy. In his book *The Gifts of the Jews: How a Tribe of Desert Nomads Changed the Way Everyone Thinks and Feels*, Thomas Cahill writes that "theirs is the only new idea that human beings have ever had."[1]

How did this new idea arise? The faithful Jew would say it was not because of the Jewish people's intelligence or creativity but because the God of Abraham chose them and guarded them as the apple of his eye. Their very existence after so many persecutions and so many years without a land witnesses to the mercy of God, who never takes back his choice. Nothing explains their unique history better than the fact that God entered the world through them, as nothing could explain the handprint on the blackboard better than the fact that someone certainly had entered that classroom.

There is another group of people dispersed throughout the world who belong to one another with an attachment deeper than nationality or culture or even ethnic origin. These are Christians. The newness of Jesus Christ and the Church is the flowering of the newness whose seeds are found in Abraham and his people.

Now that we have seen the Jews' unique history as the badge that marks them as the chosen people, let's look at the documentation. Once I find it reasonable to believe that the one true God entered into history by entering into relationship with the Jewish people, the next logical questions is, "What did he do? What did he say?"

FOR REFLECTION:

1. What, in my own personal experience, verifies the claim that I am made in the image of God?

2. Does the history of the Jewish people verify the claim that they are chosen by God?

3. Why is it important for me to verify what is revealed by our Christian faith?

CHAPTER TWO

God and Man: Two Creation Stories

Jewish history begins with the call of Abraham in Genesis 12:1. So what is going on in Genesis 1—11? In these first chapters we have stories through which the Jews consider the beginnings of human history, the genesis of all people.

The Jewish stories of the beginning of the world bear certain resemblances to myths of other ancient peoples, particularly those of Babylon, where Jews were exiled from approximately 586 to 538 BC. These similarities with myths that preceded the Old Testament do not lessen our awe of the Jewish people, for if the Jews revised these myths, the revisions themselves are evidence of a new and unique vision of the world. While other peoples speak of gods, the Jews always speak of one God. While others imagine the cosmos as a byproduct of wars among gods and humans as made from the flesh of defeated gods, the Jews proclaim that God created the world purposefully out of his goodness and created humans in his own image.[1]

Let us now confront the fact that the Old Testament begins with not one but two creation stories. The first creation story is Genesis 1:1—2:3, and the second is Genesis 2:4–25.

If you read through these two stories, you will notice that they do not agree on the order in which things were created. In the first story God creates light, sky, land, sea, vegetation, sun, moon, stars, sea creatures, birds, land animals and, at last, humans in his image, male and female. In the second story God creates earth, heavens, human male from dust, trees, land animals, birds and then human female from the male's rib.

It is at this point that I ask my students if both stories can be true. Those who are hoping to make a good impression will either take no position or say yes because they think that will make the priest happy. Those who immediately say "No!" are those who have the honesty and simplicity to learn something new, and the class becomes exciting when the first group lets down their guard and follows the second.

Certainly, if these stories are trying to express empirical science, they cannot both be true. However, these stories are revealing a deeper truth, the truth of who we are and who God is. The Jews, having encountered the living God, are in a unique position to reveal both of these truths to the world.

WHO ARE WE?

Note that the main difference in the stories' orders of creation is the place of the human. In the first story man and woman are the culmination of God's creation. Everything leads up to the human being, and in case that position of importance isn't noticed, we are told very explicitly that "God created humankind in his image," both male and female (Genesis 1:27).

In the second story, on quite the other hand, God creates men and women at different moments. He makes the man from dust and the woman later from the man's rib. Made from dust? Actually, we are told that the whole surface of the ground had been watered, so perhaps it was mud or clay that God used. But whatever it was, it wasn't glamorous. In fact, it was the same mud that God would use later to make the animals (see Genesis 2:6–7, 19).

Where is this "second story" man's dignity? The woman, coming from the side of this mud man, can't boast too much either.

The first story gives us humans as the pinnacle of all creation, made in God's very image, and the second story humbles us with Mr. and Mrs. Mud, the clay couple. There seems to be an unbridgeable abyss between these two opposing descriptions of the human person, until you look at your own human experience.

A little reflection recognizes that we are strange creatures who have a limitless desire housed within all kinds of severe limitations. Our unending and infinite desire for truth, beauty, justice and love points to the very reasonable possibility that we indeed carry in our very being something divinely limitless, the image of God. At the same time the limits that seem to compromise every other aspect of our lives make the image of dust or mud or clay seem quite appropriate. Both of these descriptions are true if taken together, and each would be a dangerous lie if it were not told alongside the other.

For example, if all we have is the claim that man bears the image of God, then I am the pinnacle of creation, and I can treat the rest of creation, including myself and other human beings, as I please. Whoever has the most power—that is, whoever seems to have the most of God's image—wins.

Might makes right. You then can have a world of slavery, oppression, abortion and euthanasia. You have a world in which science can play God. Who is to stop the glorious and godly human persons from doing whatever their desires and abilities enable them to do?

If, on the other hand, all we have is the description of the second story and humans are nothing but mud, then we can treat one another in whatever way is most expedient. We again can justify slavery, oppression, abortion and euthanasia. We have a world that reduces man to mere physical matter, where every human problem has a technical solution.

Both stories together reveal the truth of who I am and who you are and thus give me a true position from which to live. For I am made in the image of God, but I am also a creature of God, so I am not the center of the universe or even of my own life. It is true that those around me have all kinds of limits. However, along with those limits exist persons who bear the image of God. Thus I must respect every life, no matter how weak or unattractive, as something sovereign, inviolable, holy. When we see the image of God alongside the dust and the dust alongside the image of God, there is no room for exalting the human person beyond his creatureliness or reducing him to biological or psychological measures.

The most adequate and paradigmatic stance before the human person is the cross of Jesus Christ. Jesus sees human persons as worth dying for, because we bear the image of God and have a divine destiny; Jesus sees human persons as needing his death and resurrection, because our sin, our limits, cry out for a savior. Jesus reveals the way the mysterious human person is to be loved.

WHO IS GOD?

The two stories show us that man himself is a mystery, a paradox, a reality that needs to be revealed to us. As we turn our attention from God's image to God himself, we note similarly divergent descriptions.

God as described in the first story is all-powerful and mysterious. He simply says things and they happen. We never even know what he creates things from. Our human experience is that we make something new out of other things, so this God who creates from nothing is beyond what we can experience or imagine.

After God creates man, male and female, he blesses them and speaks to them, but from where is he speaking? Do the humans see him, or do they only hear him? It seems that he is speaking from the heavens, because we are told that "God saw everything that he had made" (Genesis 1:31).

Compare this omnipotent God who creates from the heavens to God in the second story, who is very clearly within the world he has created. He doesn't create by saying, "Let there be…"; he works within the created world. He creates the first man from the dust of the earth, physically forming him and breathing into his nostrils. He plants a garden. He forms animals out of the ground. He creates the woman from the rib of the man.

This God is very physical, touching everything he creates. This God will walk in the garden he has planted. He does not see everything that he has created, for when he returns to the garden, Adam and Eve are hiding from him, and he asks, "Where are you?" (Genesis 3:9). He seems to speak to Adam and Eve face-to-face. He is with them; he walks among them.

Here God is not in the heavens but on earth. He walks like us and talks like us. Even the way he creates is more similar to the way we make things: He uses his hands and works the way we work.

If all you have is the first description of God, you have a God who is distant. He could begin to resemble impersonal gods or forces, or the "unmoved mover" of Greek philosophy. If all you have is the second story, you have a God who could seem like the gods imagined by other peoples, gods who have human faces and not a lot of godliness.

What is revealed to us when we put together these two descriptions of God? God is all-powerful and exists before and beyond our limits; he wills things and they come to be. Yet he also is involved personally in his creation. He is the Lord who surveys all creation, yet he forms me in a unique and personal way. He is not a mere force; he has a face.

The first description reveals a "divine" God: mysterious, powerful, beyond. The second description reveals a very "human" God, a physical person who walks among us. A God who is divine and human? Is this what you expect in the opening pages of the Old Testament?

When we put the two descriptions of man together, we see a true revelation of who man is. When we put together the two descriptions of God, we see the beginnings of the revelation of who God is, for we have the foreshadowing of the fullness of God's revelation: Jesus Christ. The stories together show us the unimaginable mystery of God, which will be fully revealed in a way we can see and touch at the Incarnation, the literal unity of divine and human.

THE PROMISE OF SOMETHING NEW

From the beginning of the Old Testament, God is revealed to have divine and human attributes. This description of God awakens a desire and points to a promise that is fulfilled only in Jesus Christ. The desire is uttered by the psalmist: "When shall I come and behold the face of God?" (Psalm 42:2).

God certainly makes himself known in the Old Testament through the likes of Moses and David and the prophets, but Adam and Eve saw their Creator face-to-face and walked with him. This is the longing of the human heart that Jesus fulfills. When Philip says to Jesus, "Lord, show us the Father, and we shall be satisfied," Jesus replies, "Whoever has seen me has seen the Father" (John 14:8–9).

Notice that I speak now of the first description we have of God, not the first *two* descriptions. For the two creation stories are no more separable than the divinity and humanity of Christ. They exist together as one, and only in this way do they reveal the mystery of God and man.

Interestingly, Jesus is not only the perfect revelation of God, both beyond us and close to us; he is also the perfect revelation of man. He is God himself, but he took on our limits. He became like us in all things but sin. Thus the Church teaches that Christ "fully reveals man to himself."[2] He witnesses to us what it is to be fully human. In the Church's funeral liturgy, Jesus is described as the "promise and image of what we shall be."[3]

FOR REFLECTION:

1. Can science prove everything that is true?

2. Does science prove the most important truths for my life?

3. The two creation stories are not attempting to explain our existence in a scientific way. Does this make them less significant? Does this make their claims less verifiable?

CHAPTER THREE

Adam and Eve
and Jesus and Mary

When I was about nine years old, I discovered that my grandfather had a brother whom I had never been told about. When I first heard him mentioned, I was in utter disbelief. Then I assumed that he had died a long time ago, and I was even more shocked to find out that he was still alive and that we shouldn't talk about him in front of Grandpa. You see, my grandfather and his brother had a big fight, years before I was born, and they were never again on speaking terms.

When I was twenty-four years old, my grandfather died. At the evening wake, in walked a man who looked exactly like my grandfather. I knew immediately that this had to be the uncle I never had met. After he prayed at the casket, someone introduced him to me, and we proceeded to have an awkward but polite conversation. It was bizarre to speak to a man who had the face of my grandpa but was a stranger. I wanted to embrace him with all the love I had had for my grandfather, but I restrained myself because I just had met the man.

This experience helps me to understand original sin, which is not something we did but a sad condition into which we were born. It's not my fault that my uncle was a stranger to me; it was because of a fight that happened, a break in family unity that occurred before I was born.

We were born into the condition of original sin because of a split that occurred between our first parents and God. Because of this brokenness, we tend to look at God as a stranger. "Does he really exist? Does he really love me? Is he duping me? Can I trust him?" Going back to my grandpa's brother, imagine my being told, "Don't be afraid to embrace that man! He's your uncle!"

Jesus is the one who comes and tells us, "Look at me! Look at how I trust the Father! Look at how I love you! If you see me, you see the Father! Don't be afraid! God is your Father!"

So what did our first parents do? While the Old Testament tells this story in terms adapted to the people of its time, we do believe that it reveals the truth of how original sin occurred and how it was passed on to all of us by our first ancestor, Adam.[1] Somehow our first parents were tempted to turn away from God. How did this temptation begin? Through doubt.

DEBILITATED BY DOUBT:
ADAM AND EVE AND THE SUCCESS OF THE SERPENT

Adam and Eve were in a perfect garden with the perfect mate. When they looked at everything around them, they had no reason to doubt God's wisdom and goodness, and so to disobey God would be unreasonable. If the serpent is going to get them to disobey, he must first make them doubt that God really wants what is best for them.

The serpent convinces Eve that God is trying to keep her and Adam from becoming like him. God is not to be trusted, because he may be trying to dupe them.

In the end every personal sin begins with doubt. I doubt the goodness of the authority in my life. I doubt that anyone knows better than I what is good for me. I doubt that anyone really cares about my happiness, so I have to grab whatever I can, however I can. I give in to instinct because I doubt that there is really anything better in store for me, and so I settle for less than the love I am hoping for, the love I am made for. I doubt God, and I doubt the family and friends God has given me.

As soon as the first sin occurred, doubt began to flourish. It infected Adam and Eve's relationship with God. A certain familiarity was lost. Adam and Eve hid themselves from God. They were ashamed to be naked in front of him, as if he would be repulsed by his own creation. Thus they doubted that God could love them as they were. They didn't repent for their sin but placed blame elsewhere, for they doubted God's mercy. Adam even seems to have placed blame with God: "The woman whom you gave to be with me, she gave me fruit from the tree, and I ate" (Genesis 3:12). Thus Adam doubted God himself.

SALVATION OF CERTAINTY:
JESUS AND MARY AND THE CRUSHING OF THE SERPENT

The devil will use the tactic of inserting doubt again when he encounters Jesus, the New Adam, not in a garden but in a desert, where it can be much easier to doubt the goodness of God. Here the devil prefaces his temptations by saying, "If you are the Son of God…" (see Matthew 4:3, 6; Luke 4:3, 9). He wants Jesus to doubt his filial union with God, to doubt God's fatherhood and fatherly love, to break the unity of the Trinity. The devil is like the predator who knows he cannot harm the young child unless he separates the child from his parents.

How does Jesus respond to this temptation? He answers the devil with great *certainty* in his Father. This certainty is the first thing people noticed about Jesus. In the synagogue in Capernaum, "they were astounded at his teaching, for he taught them as one having authority, and not as the scribes" (Mark 1:22). What was so new about Jesus was this certainty, which Adam's heirs had never seen or experienced.

This is the same certainty with which God responds to the doubt and blaming of Adam and Eve. He justly holds the man, the woman and the serpent accountable for the sin and explains the consequences (see Genesis 3:14–19). In the midst of this stern declaration is a promise filled with a mercy that neither the man, the woman nor the serpent could have expected or imagined.

THE FIRST GOSPEL

Tradition calls Genesis 3:15 the "proto-evangelium," the "first gospel," because it is the first announcement of the coming of Jesus:

> I will put enmity between you and the woman,
>   and between your offspring and hers;
> he will strike your head,
>   and you will strike his heel.

The Church sees this strange sentence as the promise of mercy. It shines like a star within the harsh torrent of justice. The woman and her offspring are a prophecy of Mary and Jesus. In John's Gospel Jesus twice calls Mary "woman," a unique and strange way for a son to address his mother. This happens first at the beginning of Jesus' public ministry, at the wedding feast in Cana. Mary tells Jesus that there is no more wine, and Jesus responds, "Woman, what concern is that to you and to me?" (John 2:4). Mary reflects the certainty of her son when she tells the waiters to "do whatever he tells you" (John 2:5).

Mary's certainty and Jesus' subsequent miracle signal the beginning of the end of the reign of sin. For the doubt that infected the relationship that Adam and Eve (and all their heirs!) had with one another and with God is vanquished by the certainty and trust Mary and Jesus share with the Father.

The next time Jesus calls Mary "woman" is at the definitive defeat of sin: the cross. "When Jesus saw his mother and the disciple whom he loved standing beside her, he said to his mother, 'Woman, here is your son.' Then he said to the disciple, 'Here is your mother'" (John 19:26–27).

At the cross Jesus witnesses to his certainty before all creation. The Beloved Son shows that no circumstance, even suffering that leads to death, is a reason to doubt the Father, who holds all creation in his loving hands. It is here that Jesus shakes the world and urgently reveals to us that God is our Father, whom we always can embrace and trust. Jesus' certainty at the cross will be verified at the Resurrection; and doubt, the devil's currency, will be shown to be the bankrupt lie that it always was.

In giving Mary into the care of his beloved disciple at the cross, Jesus invites all his disciples into this relationship of certainty that he shares with his heavenly Father and his human mother. He makes it possible for all of us, tainted by the doubt that is the source and fruit of original sin, to enter into the unity of this family, whose relationships are full of the certainty that is the only adequate response to the love of the Father. The offspring of the woman thus crushes the head of the serpent, leaving him crippled and ultimately powerless.

THE WOMAN UNTOUCHED BY THE FLOOD

But where does Mary's certainty come from, or rather, why doesn't she doubt? The Church's answer is that she is immaculately conceived, preserved from the first moment of her existence from original sin and its doubt-filled effects. She is the morning star that breaks through the darkness of human history because she is not an heir of Adam and Eve. The New Testament witnesses to this truth.

Tradition tells us that the "Beloved Apostle" is John, who wrote the fourth Gospel. The book of Revelation is also attributed to John by early fathers of the Church. This last book of the Bible takes up the imagery of the woman, the offspring and the serpent found in the first book of the Bible.

In Revelation 12 we read about a sign in heaven, a woman giving birth to a son who will rule all the nations. As she gives birth there is a dragon (later described as a serpent) who wants to devour her child. The son escapes the serpent and ascends to the throne of God. The woman is given the wings of a great eagle so that she can escape the wrath of the serpent. (By the way, the eagle is the symbol for John's Gospel, and tradition tells us that it is John who took care of Mary, the "woman," after the death, resurrection and ascension of Jesus.)

After seeing that the woman too escaped his clutches, "from his mouth the serpent poured water like a river after the woman, to sweep her away with the flood. But the earth came to the help of the woman; it opened its mouth and swallowed the river that the dragon had poured from his mouth" (Revelation 12:15–16).

Where before have we heard about a flood? Any minimally catechized child will tell you about the flood in the story of Noah's ark. The writer of Revelation is already using imagery from Genesis when he speaks of the vision of the woman and the ancient serpent. The flood image is hearkening back to that same book.

Why did the flood in Genesis come? It came to sweep away sinful humanity. And why does this flood in Revelation 12 not touch this woman? Because she has no sin!

The serpent who crushed Adam and Eve and all their heirs with doubt is himself crushed by the certainty of Jesus and Mary. The war is won, and we are delivered.

"But I will have pity on the house of Judah, and I will save them by the LORD their God; I will not save them by bow, or by sword, or by war, or by horses, or by horsemen" (Hosea 1:7). God delivers us, the heirs of the sinful doubt and doubt-filled sin of Adam and Eve, through the innocence and certainty of Jesus and Mary, the Beloved Son and the woman, the New Adam and the New Eve.

FOR REFLECTION:

1. What is the difference between the doubt of Eve, which led her to sin, and the question of Mary before the angel, "How can this be?" (Luke 1:34). Is there a way to question from a positive position?

2. Have I experienced the debilitation of doubt in personal relationships and in my relationship with God? Have I experienced certainty in these relationships? Which experience corresponds with my desire?

CHAPTER FOUR

God's Covenant With Abraham and His Promise to Sarah

Imagine two married couples. Both are pretty well off: They eat out on weekends, go to sports events and the theater and take full advantage of life in New York City (or wherever they may live; I imagine them in New York).

Couple #1 makes a resolution to better themselves: They are going to get up an hour earlier every morning and jog; they are going to spend their free time on other people, helping at soup kitchens and nursing homes on the weekends; they are going to start giving lots of their money to the poor.

I ask my students how long Couple #1's resolution will last, and the most generous prediction I have received is three months; most predict somewhere between one day and two weeks. An unusually perceptive student once told me, "It's over before they even finish saying it." (I hope that this young man's perception of God's grace will one day be as acute as his perception of human frailty.)

Next we have Couple #2. They discover that they are going to have a baby. Within the year they find themselves getting up earlier every morning, spending weekends and much of their free time on someone else, spending gobs of their money on someone else—that is, offering their lives for another. When I ask my students how long this will last, I am told anywhere from eighteen years to forever.

Next I ask the students which of these couples is a better illustration of Christianity, and the class usually splits on their answers. Before reading on, why don't you stop and decide which of these couples you think is a better paradigm for Christianity, and think of reasons for your answer. This will tell you much about your understanding of Christianity.

Once the students have argued and voted, I explain that those who chose Couple #1 as their Christian models would have to say that Christianity can be lived for no more than three months and perhaps not really at all. I suspect that many people who have alienated themselves from the Church are Couple #1-ers who have honestly assessed that they cannot live what they perceive to be Christianity.

Once I violently erase from the board "Couple #1" and the insidious view of Christianity they represent (hoping this will not traumatize their young supporters), I explain that Couple #2 is the paradigm of Christianity. They are making all the sacrifices that Couple #1 tried to make with their own good efforts, but Couple #2's sacrifices are easy and lasting because this baby, this new person who has entered their lives, changes them and calls forth from them a previously unknown wellspring of love.

The essence of Christianity is not that I can do good on my own and please God and deserve my way into heaven. This perception is prevalent and poisonous—and heretical!

A heresy in the early Church called Pelagianism held the view that I am capable of observing God's law all by myself.

We fall into this heresy when we think that if I do really well, I go straight to heaven; if I do OK then I spend time in purgatory; and if the bad deeds outweigh the good, well, then.... It's like a big Santa list; the problem is that I am not able to be good for goodness' sake!

The fact of the matter is that I need to be moved by a presence. Christianity is the event that a new and unexpected presence enters my life. Think of a woman who falls head over heels in love with a man. Think of how she is changed when he speaks to her, invites her on a date, proposes marriage to her. (Jesus did describe himself, after all, as the Bridegroom of the Church.)

Saint John tells us, "In this is love, not that we loved God but that he loved us and sent his Son to be the atoning sacrifice for our sins" (1 John 4:10). In front of Jesus, the Incarnation of God's love, I experience a love that awakens in me an affection for him and a desire to love and sacrifice that I never before could imagine. This is what Jesus means when he says, "My yoke is easy, and my burden is light" (Matthew 11:30), and, "Apart from me you can do nothing" (John 15:5). The very thing we celebrate at Christmas is the coming of a new baby who awakens within us a completely new love and life, and all of us are invited to be Couple #2.

With their emphasis on law, it could be easy to think of the chosen people of the Old Testament as Couple #1, but this is not so. With Jesus something new certainly enters the world, but a look at the covenant with Abraham shows us that from the beginning the chosen people are pregnant with the newness that comes to us in Jesus Christ.

THE COVENANT WITH ABRAHAM

God promises Abraham his own land and numerous descendants, probably the two things most desired by a nomad. Thus we see what it means that God enters history: He does not wait for us to find our way to him but comes to us as we are, through the very things that are most important to us. Heaven has made itself present in the very earthly desires of Abraham. We also see this unity of the heavenly and earthly in the familiarity evident in the dialogues between God and Abraham.

After twice hearing about the great nation and numerous descendants that will come from him, Abraham wonders aloud to God how this will be possible, since he is childless. After God promises him land a third time, Abraham is not too shy to ask, "O Lord God, how am I to know that I shall possess it?" (Genesis 15:8). God's response is a new revelation of who he is and who we are in relation to him.

Among the peoples of the ancient Middle East, parties to a covenant promised their faithfulness to that covenant in a ritual. They would split animals in half, lay the halves across from one another, making two lines, and have each of the parties walk the path between the halves. The gesture would seem to imply that should either of the parties violate the covenant, that party should end up like those sacrificed animals.

God communicates with Abraham within his cultural context. He asks Abraham to fetch animals and split them so that God may give evidence of his faithfulness to his promise. What happens next is pivotal. Abraham falls into a deep sleep, in which God repeats his promise and prophesies the slavery of Abraham's descendants in Egypt and the Exodus that will follow. Then Abraham sees a smoking fire pot and flaming torch pass through the split animals—not unlike the pillar of cloud and fire by which the Lord would lead his people out of Egypt. Thus the "LORD made a covenant with Abram" (Genesis 15:18). For God walks through the split animals in the form of smoke and flame.

Nowhere in the text, however, does it say that Abraham walks through the animals! Abraham is in a deep sleep. Only God walks through the animals; thus the covenant rests on God's faithfulness alone. The unfaithfulness of Abraham's descendants cannot break it.

In not requiring or even allowing Abraham to walk through the animals, God mercifully acknowledges before Abraham the weakness of us humans who cannot remain faithful to our promises. God reveals to Abraham his own steadfast love by walking through alone, saying in essence, "I will be faithful to my promise, and when you and your descendants are not faithful to the promise, it is I who will be sacrificed that the covenant may be honored."

Jesus will end up being sacrificed to restore the covenant broken by our sin and to witness to God's steadfast love and fulfilled promises. When Jesus forgives his persecutors even as they are killing him (see Luke 23:34), he is revealing his Father. The Father does not wait for us to deserve his love but loves us first.

We glimpse already, in this strange covenant with Abraham, the new and unimagined love of God, which will be fulfilled in the gift of Jesus. God has a great gift awaiting his people, and like any affectionate father who has a beautiful gift to give his beloved children, our Father allows his people hints and peeks long before Christmas.

Interestingly, it was Abraham who acquired and prepared the animals that God used to reveal the newness of his love, as it is we who provide and prepare the bread and wine that become the very presence of Christ in the Eucharist. Earth and heaven, which meet in the Mass, and the human and divine, which are married in Jesus, are already engaging in a courtship with one another in the time of Abraham.

THE OLD TESTAMENT TRINITY

Another pivotal moment in the history of God's revelation involves both Abraham and Sarah. God's revelatory relationship with Sarah begins with his visit to Abraham and Sarah at their tent by the oaks of Mamre, and the way God appears is quite mysterious.

After Genesis 18:1 tells us that the Lord appeared to Abraham, something very strange happens in Genesis 18:2: Abraham "looked up and saw three men standing near him." Wait, it doesn't stop there! Read the rest of Genesis 18 and take note of the pronouns used to refer to the Lord. In verse 2 the threesome are referred to as "them," then in verse 3 Abraham refers to these three as "my Lord." Through verse 9 they are "they," but in verses 5 and 9 they even speak as one. Then in verse 10 they become "the Lord."

Is God one? Are they three? Is he three? Are they one? What's going on? Is there an editor? This is way more confusing than those two creation stories!

While those two creation stories foreshadow the Incarnation, this vision of Abraham seems to point toward the mystery of three Persons in one God, the Trinity. In fact, this mysterious vision is sometimes referred to as the Old Testament Trinity. The Church's contemplation of the gospel of Jesus Christ under the guidance of the Holy Spirit will manifest this mystery.

SARAH'S LAUGHTER

Another new revelation of the mystery of God's love occurs when the Lord tells Abraham that in the spring Sarah will have a son. Sarah hears this from inside the tent and laughs to herself, because at her age this promise seems impossible. The Lord asks why Sarah laughed, and Sarah denies having laughed. The Lord responds to this denial by saying, "No, but you did laugh," and then he leaves the tent.

Any classroom teacher will recognize this scene. How many times do students talk or laugh or turn around in class, only to deny their actions to the teacher who just saw them do it! Fighting with the student never works, but I have found that simply stating that you know you are being lied to and moving on with the class is often effective. It cuts through the excuses and goes straight to the student's heart, sometimes eliciting an apology after class, and this can be the seed of a true relationship.

God's stern "No, but you did laugh" shows the great teacher that he is. How must Sarah have been affected by that response? She must have been stunned, for don't forget that she laughed to herself! She must have been humiliated to have been caught in a lie.

As with Adam and Eve and the serpent, God recognizes Sarah's doubt and responds to it quite sternly. This God who has entered history reveals to Sarah that he desires his chosen people to relate to him in sincerity and truth. He hates lies and excuses, which put an obstacle between him and the person whom he has chosen.

You wonder if Abraham came back to the tent after seeing the Lord on his way and said to Sarah, "Well, honey, thanks a lot, there goes the baby!" Perhaps not, since Abraham also laughed when God made the same promise to him on a previous encounter (see Genesis 17:15–17).

You wonder if Sarah might have been saying such things to herself. Was she merely regretful or truly repentant? Did she desire to run after the Lord and ask forgiveness? Did she pray to him?

Whatever Sarah's personal response, clearly God has now penetrated her to the core, as he has already done with Abraham. This is what Jesus will do with everyone he encounters, from the apostles to the Pharisees to the tax collectors and sinners.

We now move forward to Genesis 21:1: "The LORD dealt with Sarah as he had said, and the LORD did for Sarah as he had promised." This one verse is perhaps the most important and revelatory in the entire Old Testament, pointing to something new in history: Sarah laughed at God and lied to God, and God fulfilled his promise! He didn't crush her; he didn't walk away and ignore her; he didn't even withdraw his promise.

This God is unlike what anyone has imagined. This God transcends all merely human notions of justice. His ways are infinitely beyond human ways. His love is so great that it will not be stopped by our doubt and sin. Sarah's greatness is that she recognizes this when she bears Isaac and exclaims, "God has brought laughter for me; everyone who hears will laugh with me" (Genesis 21:6).

Sarah's laughter is for everyone, because Sarah has discovered that God fulfills his promise even when we are not worthy. God loves us not because we are good but because he is unimaginably good. When a world wracked with fearsome images of gods hears about this, it too will have reason to laugh. That Sarah's sin did not stop God from showing her his love is just as miraculous as the fruit borne by her elderly womb. Sarah has discovered what will later be revealed to Mary when the angel promises the coming of Jesus: "Nothing will be impossible with God" (Luke 1:37).

ECHOES OF LAUGHTER

It can seem as if Adam and Eve did not receive the same favor as Sarah. It seems that they were punished for their doubt and sin. However, when we recall the promise God gave them of the woman and her offspring, which will be fulfilled in Jesus, we see that all of salvation history follows the same path of what happened to Sarah that beautiful spring. God responds to sin with mercy. Sarah shows us what is required of the sinner: truthfulness and joyful recognition and acceptance of mercy when it is offered.

In fact, this wonderful exchange between God and Sarah may have been the seed of the familiar relationship the chosen people would enjoy with God, evidenced in the psalms of lament referred to in chapter one. Recall how the Jews pray to God and complain to God with complete sincerity and with the confidence that God's desire is not to condemn them for their sins but to carry them with mercy to the fulfillment of their destiny.

The birth of Isaac, the fulfillment of the promise to both Abraham and Sarah despite their doubt, also must have sustained the Jews during difficult periods of their history. Imagine a Jew tempted to lose hope during slavery in Egypt repeating to himself, "Sarah had a son! Sarah had a son! I know God will not disappoint us, because Sarah laughed and lied and Sarah had a son!"

Recall the Jewish notion of memory. The Passover, which remembers and makes present the Exodus, and the Mass, which remembers and makes present the death and resurrection of Christ, are both repeated for this very reason: that we never make the grave mistake of losing hope in God, whose mercy endures forever and is present and operative now.

How sad that so many people imagine God to be like a stern judge, ready to condemn us with our long list of evil deeds. This is not the God Jesus Christ revealed, and this is not, as many mistakenly believe, the God the Old Testament reveals to us. God made a covenant with Abraham that God would keep. Abraham merely had to say yes and trust in God's promise.

God's goodness is verified in the fruit that comes forth from the womb of Sarah. The very existence of Isaac is a sign, in the flesh, that God keeps his promises to his people, even when his people falter. For God knows who we are, and he comes among us to show us who he is.

In the next chapter we will see that the fruit of Sarah's womb foreshadows the fruit of Mary's womb in more ways than one.

FOR REFLECTION:

1. Have I experienced Christianity as an encounter with Christ through another person?

2. Can I point to changes that have happened to me as a result of this encounter, changes that never could have happened through merely following rules?

3. What are the greatest experiences of mercy in my life?

CHAPTER FIVE

The Sacrifice of a Beloved Son

It is not possible for a Christian to live in modern, secular culture and not be affected by it. The predominant mentality has ways of inserting itself into our ways of seeing things. Thus I sometimes find a tendency in myself and among other Catholics to think of God as somehow not as enlightened as we are. It is as if God were a doddering old man who just doesn't get it, and he would do better if he would only take our advice and see things from our enlightened point of view. We fashion God as a kind of grandpa who is endearing but irrelevant.

This would seem to be the basis of those who feel the need to reinterpret God's revelation to better fit current problems, which we understand "oh so much better" than anyone before us could have. The doddering God is also the image of those whose practice of the faith is reduced to "God gave me so much, I figure I could at least give him an hour a week." Going to church becomes kind of like a weekly visit to the nursing home.

As the elderly grandparent might say strange things that we don't understand, so at Mass we might hear God revealing some strange stuff, especially in the Old Testament readings.

The elderly ancestor can anger us with his old-fashioned closed-mindedness, or we can nod our heads kindly and leave the visit unaffected by what we see as his ramblings. So also there are people who shake their heads at certain readings at Mass and put themselves into the very frightening position of judging God, while others kindly ignore difficult passages or make little jokes about them and move on.

Perhaps no story in the Bible provokes these kinds of reactions more than that of God's asking Abraham to sacrifice Isaac. This is particularly interesting since Abraham's attitude toward God in this passage could not be further from either of these reductive ways of conceiving of him.

ABRAHAM AND HIS SON ON THE MOUNTAIN

It is clear that for Abraham, God is everything. Abraham knows that he is the man he is because God has entered his life. God is the source of Abraham's hope, for he is the source of the promises that correspond to the desires of Abraham's heart. It is not that God has given Abraham "so much" but that God has given him everything, and everything includes Isaac. For Abraham and Sarah did not deserve Isaac; their son was a gift of God.

Let us also note that Abraham, like us, lived in a time and place that affected his mentality. It was not uncommon for other peoples to sacrifice their children to gods; and in the end, when God spares Isaac, he could be showing Abraham something new: that God is not requiring his people to sacrifice their children to him. God is revealing himself to be completely different from the gods imagined and fashioned by the peoples of the Middle East at that time.

This in itself is quite a revelation. And yet, when we read

this passage in the light of Christ, we see that God is revealing much more.

God says to Abraham, "Take your son, your only son Isaac, whom you love, and go to the land of Moriah, and offer him there as a burnt offering on one of the mountains that I shall show you" (Genesis 22:2). We can think that Abraham is a terrible father for not refusing or arguing, but again, Abraham has an acute sense that everything comes from God and that God can be trusted.

When Abraham gets to the mountain, he has Isaac carry the wood for the offering. Isaac asks his father, "Where is the lamb for a burnt offering?" to which Abraham responds, "God will himself provide the lamb." At the top of the mountain, just as Abraham takes the knife to slay his son, God says to him, "Do not lay your hand on the boy or do anything to him; for now I know that you fear God, since you have not withheld your son, your only son, from me" (see Genesis 22:7–8, 12).

How many of us really think of our children, our friends or our family as gifts of God? When people get angry at God because of the death of their loved ones, do they ever think about the fact that without God, their beloved would never have existed? And that God is their only hope that their beloved still does exist?

We tend to think of the world as having "been there." God sort of comes along as the custodian of what was already there and rightfully ours. We need to realize that God is the source of everything. There is simply nothing "there" without God's goodness, and everything that exists is a free gift of God and a sign of his presence.

Even if we are aware of all this, the scene of Abraham and Isaac on the mountain can be profoundly disturbing. For we are human, and God has created in us a strong bond with our children and an undying love for them. God's request to Abraham to offer his own son to God, even knowing that son came from God, seems unfair. To sacrifice the joy of one's heart seems too much to do, too much to give, too much to even imagine.

We recoil in horror at this passage in Genesis, despite any arguments for its legitimacy. If we keep in mind this very human response of our own heart to Abraham's sacrifice, it becomes a window into the heart of God and the love of God.

GOD THE FATHER AND HIS SON ON THE MOUNTAIN

As the first creation story is incomplete without the second, the sacrifice of Abraham and Isaac is incomplete without the fulfillment, which happens in the sacrifice of the Father and the Son at the cross.

God describes Isaac in Genesis 22:2 as Abraham's beloved son. Interestingly, the only time God the Father audibly speaks in the Gospels is when he calls Jesus his own "Beloved Son." The Father speaks these words from heaven at Jesus' baptism and later at the Transfiguration (see Matthew 3:17; Mark 1:11; Luke 3:22; Matthew 17:5; Mark 9:7; Luke 9:35).

As Abraham's beloved son carried the wood for sacrifice up the mountain, God's beloved Son would carry his wooden cross. Abraham's beloved son asked about the lamb of sacrifice, and Abraham told him that the lamb would be provided by God. Abraham may not have known that he was speaking prophetically, for God would provide the Lamb for the sacrifice, *his* own beloved Son, Jesus, the Lamb of God.

God spoke from the heavens to spare Isaac, but there was no such voice to stop the sacrifice of his beloved Son on Calvary. While the Father's voice was silent, nature seemed to manifest his heart as he watched his beloved Son die: darkness came over the land, the earth shook, rocks were split, the curtain of the temple was torn in two (see Matthew 27:45, 51–52; Mark 15:33, 38; Luke 23:44–45). God spared Abraham's beloved son; he sacrificed his own.

These two sacrifices seen together shed light on one another and become yet another way in which God reveals to us the depth of his love. God does for us what we could not conceive of doing for him. This God is unlike us, and he is unlike any god the pagan peoples imagined. These peoples could imagine their gods' demands for the lives of their children, but who could imagine God the Father's sacrifice of his Beloved Son for us! God's ways are not only different from ours but unimaginably contrary to our ways of thinking.

The Father's voice in the Gospels resonates with greater richness when we keep Abraham and Isaac in mind. We can hear him saying: "This is *my* Beloved Son. Abraham's beloved was spared; now see how I will sacrifice my own Beloved for you, and then you may understand my love for you. My love for you, my children, is far beyond the love you could ever have for me. It is a love infinitely greater than you could ask for or imagine or ever deserve, even with an eternity of righteous deeds."

To doubt God's goodness because of the request he made to Abraham is like doubting a parent's goodness because of the discipline the child receives. When a child grows to full stature, he understands that his parents were loving him the whole time. When the sacrifice on Abraham's mountain is fulfilled on Calvary, we understand that God has loved us at every step in his plan for our salvation and that every step mysteriously communicates this love.

In light of these two complementary events, it seems too little to say that God loves us. Psalm 8 aptly expresses God's relationship with us:

> What are human beings that you are mindful of them,
>   mortals that you care for them?
> Yet you have made them a little lower than God,
>   and crowned them with glory and honor.
> (Psalm 8:4–5)

FOR REFLECTION:

1. Have I set myself up as God's judge?

2. Do I take my life and all its benefits for granted?

3. When have I made a connection between a particular gift in my life and God as the giver?

CHAPTER SIX

Mystery Men of Old and New

Krzysztof Kieslowski was a Polish director who made a series of films inspired by each of the Ten Commandments. The main characters in the first film, *Decalogue I*, are a boy, his father and his aunt. There is a fourth character who seems to have no particular purpose. He is simply a man who sits by the side of a pond. The camera focuses every so often on this unexplained man. The director clearly has a purpose for this character, but it is not immediately evident to the viewer.

At various times I have shown this film to students ranging in age from twelve to seventeen years. The students are always fascinated by this character, if for no other reason than that he is mysterious. Frequently students have commented, "He must represent God," or, "I think he's supposed to be Jesus."

Let us leave the man at the pond to be pondered by film buffs, and let us turn our attention to three mysterious characters who exit as quickly as they enter into the Old Testament accounts of Abraham, Jacob and Joseph.

ABRAHAM AND THE KING

In Genesis 14 Abraham goes into battle against an alliance of kings because they have captured his nephew Lot. When he returns from victory, "King Melchizedek of Salem,... priest of God Most High," brings out bread and wine and blesses Abraham. Melchizedek arrives in verse 18 and completes his blessing in verse 20, never again to appear in Abraham's story.

Who is this man? He will be mentioned only once more in the Old Testament, in Psalm 110, where a Davidic king receives the promise, "You are a priest forever according to the order of Melchizedek" (Psalm 110:4).

Like the man in the film, Melchizedek becomes the topic of much discussion. The writer of the Letter to the Hebrews writes at length about him, explicitly stating that Melchizedek is made to resemble the Son of God. He points out that "King of Salem" means "King of Peace" and that Melchizedek is not only a king but also a priest, one whose priesthood will last forever (see Hebrews 7:1–3).

The resemblance between Melchizedek, the king priest who blesses with bread and wine, and Jesus, who offers bread and wine the night before his sacrifice, is so much a part of Church tradition that the mysterious Melchizedek is mentioned even in the Mass. The Roman Canon, also known as the First Eucharistic Prayer, speaks of the bread and wine "offered by your priest, Melchizedek."[1]

Melchizedek is not the only mysterious man in the Old Testament who bears a striking resemblance to Jesus. The next two men we will look at are not even given names.

Jacob and the Man

We often hear the story of Jacob's wrestling with an "angel," but in the actual Scripture passage, Genesis 32:24–32, Jacob's wrestling partner is described as a man. This man enters at verse 24, seemingly out of nowhere, and appears to be gone by verse 30.

In verse 26 Jacob asks this man for a blessing. This seems inconceivable, especially to me and my high school students. A physical assault of another student is reason for detention or suspension; you can be sure that the victim will not ask the perpetrator for his blessing. (In fact, such unfortunate encounters are normally accompanied by curses.) By asking for the man's blessing, Jacob is acknowledging that this man is somehow superior to him and somehow holy.

The man gives Jacob a new name, something that only God does. The new name is *Israel*, which means "the one who strives with God" or "God strives." Jacob has "striven with God and with humans" and has "prevailed" (Genesis 32:28).

God and humans? Is this man referring to Jacob's previous dealings with Laban and Esau? Or is he speaking of himself? Is he himself God or man? Why is *human* plural? Is this a return of Abraham's mysterious visitors?

After he receives a blessing from the man, Jacob marvels, "I have seen God face to face" (Genesis 32:30). So the mysterious wrestling partner starts out as a man and ends up being God! Who can he be?

In one class I traced through these man-to-God steps on the blackboard for the students to put in their notebooks. At the end of the outline I wrote, "A prophecy of Jesus?" One student was a bit perplexed when he finished copying. He raised his hand and wondered why there was a question mark at the end of that final phrase. In deference to his simplicity and certainty, I erased the question mark.

The stages of revelation of the wrestling partner are especially interesting because they mark the path that Jesus' disciples will take in the Gospels. At first Jesus must have seemed like any other man. The first two disciples only noticed him because John the Baptist pointed him out and said, "Here is the Lamb of God who takes away the sin of the world!" (John 1:29). After seeing the authority with which Jesus spoke and lived, the miracles he performed and the way he looked at the people he encountered, those who followed Jesus recognized him to be a holy man, perhaps a great prophet, perhaps the Messiah.

Then the disciples began to believe that Jesus was even more than this. For Jesus did things that only God can do. For instance, he told a paralytic that his sins were forgiven, and then he healed him only to give evidence that he had authority to forgive sins, an authority that the bystanders knew belonged only to God (see Matthew 9:2–8; Mark 2:3–12; Luke 5:17–26).

At a certain point Jesus' declarations of his divinity became more explicit. Particularly interesting in light of the revelation made to Jacob is Matthew 16:13–18:

> Now when Jesus came into the district of Caesarea Philippi, he asked his disciples, "Who do people say that the Son of Man is?" And they said, "Some say John the Baptist, but others Elijah, and still others Jeremiah or one of the prophets." He said to them, "But who do you say that I am?" Simon Peter answered, "You are the Messiah, the Son of the living God." And Jesus answered him, "Blessed are you, Simon son of

Jonah! For flesh and blood has not revealed this to you, but my
Father in heaven. And I tell you, you are Peter, and on this rock
I will build my church, and the gates of Hades will not prevail
against it."

Jesus verified Simon's amazing confession. Simon, like Jacob,
was in wonder that he saw God face-to-face. Like the man
wrestling with Jacob, Jesus gave Simon a new name, Peter.
In the end both Jacob and Peter prevail. And both have trav-
eled the same path: They encountered a man, they understood that man to be holy, and they ultimately understood
that man to be God.

JOSEPH AND THE MAN

We will consider in more detail later the Old Testament story
of Joseph. Here I want to look at the man Joseph encountered
on his way to see his brothers in Shechem.

We are told that "a man found [Joseph] wandering in the
fields of Shechem." This mystery man does not engage in
wrestling or bring forth bread and wine; he simply asks
Joseph, "What are you seeking?" When Joseph asks the man
the whereabouts of his brothers, the man advises him to look
in Dothan (see Genesis 37:15–17).

Why should we pay any attention to this man? He enters
Genesis 37 at verse 15 and is gone by verse 17, never to appear
in Joseph's story again. What could he matter?

That man by the pond in *Decalogue I* also seems unimportant to the story, except for the fact that the director has
chosen to include him. The director had to hire an actor, set
up shots and use precious film time in order to include this
mysterious man. No small thing.

What of the one who wrote down the story of Joseph? What of those who told the story long before it was written down? Why mention this man? Couldn't we have been told that Joseph went to Shechem and his brothers weren't there, so he continued to Dothan? This man merits attention simply because he is there!

Does this man resemble Christ? I believe he does, because the question this man asks is the same as the first question Jesus will ask his disciples (in fact, the first thing Jesus says to his first two disciples): "What are you looking for?" (John 1:38).

In the next chapter we will see many parallels between Joseph and Jesus. One parallel that does not quite fit is that Joseph is one of twelve brothers. Jesus did choose twelve disciples, but he himself was not one of the twelve. This man also is not one of the twelve, and he is the only one in the story who advises Joseph; everyone else receives Joseph's advice.

From Where Did They Come?

John's Gospel tells us of some people in Jerusalem who wondered about Jesus: "Yet we know where this man is from; but when the Messiah comes, no one will know where he is from." Jesus cries in response, "You know me, and you know where I am from" (John 7:27–28). Later he tells the Pharisees, "I know where I have come from and where I am going, but you do not know where I come from or where I am going" (John 8:14).

What unites these three mysterious Old Testament characters—Melchizedek, Jacob's wrestler and the direction-giver at Shechem—is that they all seem to come into the story from nowhere. Where did they come from? Where did they go? Why are they there?

Melchizedek is a king and a priest of God Most High. How does this fit into the Old Testament, given that he is not even a Jew and exists before the Jewish priesthood is established? The mystery continues when Psalm 110 promises a king of the line of David that he will be a priest not of the order of Aaron or of the Levites but of the order of Melchizedek (see Psalm 110:4)!

The wrestler is a man who is also God! He mysteriously appears and just as mysteriously disappears. And what about the man who gives Joseph directions? His words seem to foreshadow the words of Jesus.

Prophecies of Jesus?

(Do what you want with the question mark.) As much as Jesus is predicted and prophesied, he came as a surprise, infinitely more surprising than these three figures. No one expected God to become human. No one expected the Messiah to be as Jesus was.

The presence of Christ always carries with it an element of unpredictability and wonder. For his ways are above our ways (see Isaiah 55:9). Our faith is a living faith because we follow a living presence, not a dead set of laws or a book. This is why Catholics unabashedly proclaim that the Bible itself is not enough! The Bible itself confirms this: It contains signs of this human and divine unpredictability, as witnessed by these three mysterious presences.

The Bible—not enough? Our own human experience tells us this. We need the presence of a living person who continually surprises us and brings us beyond our preconceptions and limited expectations. A book on friendship is nice, but I need friends! An orphan might enjoy reading stories about mothers and fathers, but this can't compare with having a mother and father!

The Person of Jesus Christ is present in the Church, which is made up of living members of the body of Christ, made so by the grace of baptism and invited to remain alive in Christ through the lifeblood of the sacraments. For two thousand years Christ has remained in the world through these weak and sinful human beings who are mysteriously members of his body.

JACOB'S DREAM: A LIVING REALITY

Jacob's dream seems to foreshadow this mystical presence of Christ. This dream comes a few chapters before Jacob's encounter with the man-God wrestler. I am writing of the dream after having written of the wrestler as a gesture of my own wild unpredictability!

In the dream Jacob sees a stairway that connects heaven and earth. While Jacob beholds this stairway, the Lord tells Jacob about his descendants:

> And the LORD stood beside him and said, "I am the LORD, the God of Abraham your father and the God of Isaac; the land on which you lie I will give to you and to your offspring; and your offspring shall be like the dust of the earth, and you shall spread abroad to the west and to the east and to the north and to the south; and all the families of the earth shall be blessed in you and in your offspring. Know that I am with you and will keep you wherever you go, and will bring you back to this land; for I will not leave you until I have done what I have promised you." (Genesis 28:13–15)

Jacob sees a stairway and hears about his descendants. What is the connection between what is seen and what is heard?

One is an image of the other. God's people are the stairway—that is, the connection—between heaven and earth. God's chosen people are the physical sign of God's presence on earth.

This is true first for the Jewish people. For through the prophet Isaiah, the Lord will say, "I am the first and I am the last; / besides me there is no god.... / You are my witnesses!" (see Isaiah 44:6, 8). God chose a people to be his own, and this people would witness to God's presence because they would continue to be exceptional. Through the laws and customs they kept, they would stand out from other peoples. Even dispersed without a land, they would not assimilate. Their exceptionality would be a sign that they belonged to God.

Jesus comes as the fulfillment of the desire of the Jewish people. In John's Gospel he seems to compare himself to the stairway. As Jacob sees God's messengers ascending and descending on the stairway, so Jesus prophesies to Nathanael, "Very truly I tell you, you will see heaven opened, and the angels of God ascending and descending upon the Son of man" (John 1:51). In the union of his divinity and humanity, Jesus is the connection between heaven and earth. He is the promise of communion between God and his people.

The promise of this communion is evident today in the Christian people, the mystical body of Christ. Through their flesh animated by the gift of the Holy Spirit, God is present on earth in a real, sacramental way. Thus the connection between heaven and earth, which is the Person of Jesus Christ, remains tangible and knowable through the Church.

Recall that Jesus said, "Where two or three are gathered in my name, I am there among them" (Matthew 18:20). Christ's presence manifests itself to the world through our unity.

When Saint Paul was persecuting Christians, Jesus appeared to him and said, "Saul, Saul, why do you persecute *me*?" (Acts 9:4, emphasis added). So much does the risen Christ identify himself with his people. Saint Paul writes to the Christians in Corinth, "Now you are the body of Christ and individually members of it" (1 Corinthians 12:27). This is the fulfillment of God's promise to Jacob, "Know that I am with you" (Genesis 28:15).

Jesus is present through the unity of Christians. This unity is the strongest sign to the world that God is with us; it is how we become the connection between heaven and earth. At the Last Supper Jesus prays that his future disciples "may become completely one, so that the world may know that you have sent me" (John 17:23). The more visible our unity, the more visibly present is Christ.

In his book *Why the Church?* Monsignor Luigi Giussani points out that throughout history people have reacted to the Church in the same way that people reacted to Jesus of Nazareth, whether that reaction was acceptance or rejection.[2] The body of Christ is living and active in the world through the Church.

God promised Jacob that by his descendants all the nations on the earth would be blessed. What is a greater blessing than the discovery that God is present in a mysterious yet tangible way through a people that we can see and touch?

We began this chapter with mysterious men who somehow prophesied the presence of Jesus Christ. We end with Jacob's vision, which indicates that the mode of God's presence is his chosen people and that this connection is made perfect and permanent through Jesus Christ, who remains present in the Church. Thus you and I have become those mysterious, seemingly unimportant people whose presence in the world points to and even carries within it the very presence of God.

Living signs of Christ's presence? (Do what you want with the question mark.)

FOR REFLECTION:

1. What particular people have been Christ in my life?

2. Have I had an experience of being Christ for another person? Did this happen because of an intentional effort on my part or in another way?

CHAPTER SEVEN

Joseph and Jesus

Perhaps the most joyful moment of the year in my high school course on the Old Testament is when we go through the story of Joseph (see Genesis 37, 39—45). All the assignments are to find parallels to Jesus in the various moments of the narrative.

The inspiration of Scripture is clearly evident to me when I see the enthusiasm with which the students go after this task and how easily they remember the details of this story. The timely completion of homework reaches record highs.

The "Joseph test" at the end of the unit is to write a long essay in class on these parallels.

In this chapter I am taking that test.

If you are thinking it's unfair that I get to have the Bible open before me as I write this chapter, please refrain from such unjust accusations. I let my students have their Bibles open for their test as well. I don't want them "inventing" Jesus; I want them to learn to recognize his presence by reading what they have before them, whether it be the words of the Bible I present in my class or the people and circumstances that make up the reality that God puts before them in their lives.

I hope I do well on this test, although I am certain I will miss some points. Every time I teach this story, the students come up with insights I had not thought about before. (And every once in a while I am humble enough to admit it to them!)

BELOVED, OBEDIENT SON

All of the drama of Joseph's life goes back to one fact: Israel, his father, loves Joseph more than all of his other sons. All the drama of Jesus' human life, and the essence of his very existence, is that he is the beloved Son of God the Father.

The Incarnation is Jesus' obedience to the Father. As Joseph responded with "Here I am" when his father Israel sent him to his brothers (Genesis 37:13), Jesus came to us out of ready and loving obedience to his Father. The Letter to the Hebrews sees a passage from Psalm 40 as the words of Jesus at his incarnation:

> When Christ came into the world, he said,
> "Sacrifices and offerings you have not desired,
>   but a body you have prepared for me;
> in burnt offerings and sin offerings
>   you have taken no pleasure.
> Then I said, 'See, God, I have come to do your will, O God'
>   (in the scroll of the book it is written of me)."
> (Hebrews 10:5–7)

Israel's preference for Joseph, along with Joseph's dreams, which foreshadow his brothers' bowing down before him, cause his brothers to be jealous of him to the point of wanting him dead. In Matthew's Gospel we see this same kind of jealousy at the outset with King Herod. In fact, to avoid Herod's death sentence Joseph and Mary bring Jesus into Egypt, exactly where Israel's son Joseph ended up as the alternative to death at his brothers' hands (see Genesis 39:1; Matthew 2:13–15).

The jealousy of the scribes and Pharisees is evident in all four Gospels. One of Jesus' responses to this jealousy is the parable he tells of the tenant farmers. The landowner sends his son to the tenants, and they say to each other, "This is the heir; come, let us kill him and get his inheritance" (Matthew 21:38).

Kings and Pharisees and tenant farmers are understandably jealous of someone who threatens to displace them from their positions, but Joseph suffers at the hands of his own brothers! Jesus also knows that even those who follow him could betray him. John tells us, "When he was in Jerusalem during the Passover festival, many believed in his name because they saw the signs that he was doing. But Jesus on his part would not entrust himself to them, because he knew all people and needed no one to testify about anyone; for he himself knew what was in everyone" (John 2:23–25). In the end an apostle, one of the twelve disciples who are closest to Jesus, will betray him.

Joseph's brother Reuben convinces the brothers to throw Joseph into an empty cistern instead of killing him. Reuben plans to go back to the cistern later and rescue Joseph. The brothers strip Joseph, just as the soldiers will strip Jesus, and they throw him into the cistern.

As they eat their lunch afterward (I suppose hurling your brother toward his death leaves you hungry), the brothers see a group of Ishmaelite traders on their way to Egypt. Judah, the forebear of Jesus, convinces his brothers to sell Joseph as a slave for twenty pieces of silver. Remember that Judas will betray Jesus for thirty pieces of silver.

Poor Reuben, who apparently lunched elsewhere, comes later to the cistern to rescue Joseph, and it is empty, just as the tomb of Jesus will be found empty by Mary Magdalene, Peter and John. Later the brothers tell their father that Joseph has died, and as evidence they offer Joseph's tunic, which they have soaked in goat's blood. At hearing this Jacob tears his clothes. At Jesus' death, Mark's Gospel tells us, "the curtain of the temple was torn in two, from top to bottom" (Mark 15:38). It is as if God the Father is tearing his own robe at the death of his beloved Son.

AUTHORITY GIVEN

When Joseph arrives in Egypt, a courtier of Pharaoh named Potiphar buys him. Potiphar sees that the Lord is with Joseph, and so he entrusts everything he owns to Joseph's charge. Throughout his life the authority that Joseph exercised was given by someone else. His father sent him to his brothers, Potiphar gave him authority over his house, the chief jailer put him in charge of the other prisoners, and Pharaoh told Joseph, "Only with regard to the throne will I be greater than you" (see Genesis 37:13; 39:4, 22; 41:40).

We can see Joseph's awareness of this fact most acutely when Potiphar's wife tries to seduce him. Joseph tells her, "Look, with me here, my master has no concern about anything in the house, and he has put everything that he has in my hand. He is not greater in this house than I am, nor has he kept back anything from me except yourself, because you are his wife. How then could I do this great wickedness, and sin against God?" (Genesis 39:8–9). For Joseph the greatest wickedness of the sin into which he is being invited is not the adultery itself but the betrayal of the one who has entrusted him with his authority.

We can see in these incidents images of the Father entrusting everything to Jesus. At the end of Matthew's Gospel Jesus says, "All authority in heaven and on earth has been given to me" (Matthew 28:18). In his Letter to the Ephesians, Saint Paul writes that God the Father "has put all things under [Jesus'] feet and has made him the head over all things for the church, which is his body, the fullness of him who fills all in all" (Ephesians 1:22–23).

Jesus' awareness that he acts in the name of the Father is especially explicit in the Gospel of John. At one point Jesus tells the Pharisees, "I do nothing on my own, but I speak these things as the Father instructed me" (John 8:28). He knew "that the Father had given all things into his hands" (John 13:3).

Joseph's faithfulness to Potiphar and Jesus' faithfulness to his Father do not spare them suffering. The temptations Jesus endures in the desert all have to do with distrusting and betraying the Father (see Matthew 4:1–11; Luke 4:1–13). Both Joseph and Jesus are accused falsely and thrown into prison, and Jesus is tortured and crucified. However, Joseph's faithfulness brings him to the point where he is able to save his brothers from famine, and Jesus' faithfulness brings him to his passion, death and resurrection, in which he saves us.

Doubt and betrayal of the Father are the source of all evil, even if they seem immediately gratifying. Trust in and faithfulness to the Father are the source of all good, even though they may entail suffering and sacrifice.

TWO PRISONERS, TWO THIEVES

Having been falsely accused by Potiphar's wife, Joseph finds himself in prison, where he interprets the dreams of a cupbearer and a baker. I must speak about the cupbearer and baker in faithfulness to one of my students, George, who noticed a parallel that I hadn't seen.

You see, Joseph tells the cupbearer that he will live and return to his cupbearing position, while Joseph tells the baker that he will be impaled on a stake, and the birds will peck at his flesh. George compared these two prisoners to the two thieves crucified at Jesus' side. One repents and lives (like the cupbearer), and the other, well…(kind of like the baker).

I am sure others have seen this parallel and even written about it, and maybe I shouldn't admit that it did not jump out at me or that I have not read as extensively as I should have, but there you have it. (And this is why teaching is exciting!)

Something else interesting happens in this scene. (Now that George has put us on the trail, why not walk it all the way!) For a moment the cupbearer seems to be a type of Christ, and Joseph seems to be a type of the good thief. For the cupbearer is told he will return to Pharaoh "within three days" (Genesis 40:13). Joseph asks the cupbearer to remember him to Pharaoh in order to get him out of prison. This is reminiscent of the good thief's asking Jesus to remember him when he comes into his kingdom.

The cupbearer, unfortunately, forgets all about Joseph until Pharaoh starts having bad dreams and wants an interpreter. Then the cupbearer, who also seems to be a master of understatement, suddenly recalls that there is a man suffering in prison who did him a good turn and asked him for one simple favor. "I remember my faults today," he says (Genesis 41:9). This is a great reminder to all of us that types of Jesus are always only types of Jesus; only Jesus is Jesus.

RECOGNITION AND RESURRECTION

Joseph sees that Pharaoh's dream means seven years of feast followed by seven years of famine, and he wisely plans to put plenty of food in storage. At that point Jacob sends his sons to Egypt to buy food. There are two separate journeys full of details that you will find in Genesis 42—44 (and that my poor students are responsible to remember). What interests us here is the fact that the brothers do not recognize Joseph when they see him—on either journey!

Three times in the Gospels, the disciples do not recognize the risen Jesus: Mary Magdalene thinks he is the gardener when she meets him at the tomb (see John 20:15); the disciples on the road to Emmaus think he is just a fellow traveler (Luke 24:16); and the apostles do not recognize him when he is standing on the shore (John 21:4–7).

Mary Magdalene's moment of recognizing Jesus is the one most similar to the brothers' recognition of Joseph. In both cases it is a decided revelation on the part of Joseph and Jesus. They each reveal themselves because they are moved by an act of love they see happening before them.

In Joseph's case Judah has offered to give himself as a slave in order to free his brother Benjamin. Joseph is so moved by this act of sacrifice that he "could no longer control himself" (Genesis 45:1). He has all his attendants leave the room and reveals himself to his brothers. His first concern is to ask about his father.

Jesus similarly is moved by the love of Mary Magdalene. She thinks he is the gardener and asks him where he has taken the body of Jesus so that she can go and take it. Her love for Jesus shows little regard for her own limitations, for surely she would not have the physical strength to move the body alone.

Jesus reveals himself to Mary by saying her name. Mary clings to Jesus, whereupon he says, "Do not hold on to me, because I have not yet ascended to the Father" (John 20:17). Like Joseph, Jesus' first consideration is for his Father.

Why does Jesus appear to his disciples in a way they do not recognize? What purpose did this serve?

I think he did this for us. This goes back to what we spoke of at the end of chapter six. Jesus remains present through the Church, which means that today I encounter Christ through faces that don't look like him. What seems like a gardener, or some guy on the road, or some guy on the beach, or my husband or wife or friend or son or daughter or coworker, is the mode of Christ's presence to me. Yes, only Jesus is Jesus, but Jesus' desire is to be with us in the flesh. In a mysterious way our flesh is his flesh, so much do we belong to him.

Mary Magdalene recognized Jesus when he said her name, the disciples on the road to Emmaus recognized him when he broke the bread, and the disciples in the boat recognized him when they caught a miraculous load of fish at his direction. They all recognized Jesus not by his physical features but by his gestures. Unity with Jesus is unity with those whose gestures make me recognize him.

The more in union I am with Jesus, the more my own flesh vibrates with his presence, even to the point that Saint Paul describes, "It is no longer I who live, but it is Christ who lives in me. And the life I now live in the flesh I live by faith in the Son of God, who loved me and gave himself for me" (Galatians 2:20).

MERCY

Luigi Giussani once said that mercy is God's ability to bring good out of bad.[1] This is the most important parallel between the life of Joseph and the life of Jesus.

Joseph's brothers are sorrowful and fearful before him because of their betrayal. Twice Joseph reassures them:

> Then Joseph said to his brothers, "Come closer to me." And they came closer. He said, "I am your brother, Joseph, whom you sold into Egypt. And now do not be distressed, or angry with yourselves, because you sold me here; for God sent me before you to preserve life. For the famine has been in the land these two years; and there are five more years in which there will be neither plowing nor harvest. God sent me before you to preserve for you a remnant on earth, and to keep alive for you many survivors. So it was not you who sent me here, but God; he has made me a father to Pharaoh, and lord of all his house and ruler over all the land of Egypt." (Genesis 45:4–8)
>
> "Even though you intended to do harm to me, God intended it for good, in order to preserve a numerous people, as he is doing today. So have no fear; I myself will provide for you and your little ones." In this way he reassured them, speaking kindly to them. (Genesis 50:20–21)

Joseph's brothers sold him into slavery! Out of this heinous evil God brings all the good that Joseph did. Thousands of lives are saved because of Joseph's unlikely journey into

Egypt. God looked upon a journey begun through evil and mercifully begot a way that led to good.

It is the mystery of God's mercy that leads the Church to speak of the sin of Adam as a "happy fault."[2] Jesus utters this mystery from the cross as he prays for the very people who are crucifying him, "Father, forgive them; for they do not know what they are doing" (Luke 23:34). Saint Paul writes,

> For just as by the one man's disobedience the many were made sinners, so by the one man's obedience the many will be made righteous. But law came in, with the result that the trespass multiplied; but where sin increased, grace abounded all the more, so that, just as sin exercised dominion in death, so grace might also exercise dominion through justification leading to eternal life through Jesus Christ our Lord. (Romans 5:19–21)

I speak of this mystery in preparing couples for marriage. I tell them that even their betrayals of one another will not be obstacles to their unity but a help. When I betray or fail someone and that person forgives me, I discover a depth of their love for me that I didn't know before the betrayal. This doesn't mean that I want intentionally to betray, and it doesn't mean that I am not sorry for my betrayals. Perhaps I cannot easily explain this mysterious truth, but I know it from experience.

God's mercy is so pervasive that he even uses our sins to bring forth his good. When I am truly repentant and receive God's forgiveness, my sins actually become stepping stones on my path toward communion with the Father.

GOD WITH US

When Joseph was about to die, he said to his brothers, "God will surely come to you, and bring you up out of this land to the land that he swore to Abraham, to Isaac, and to Jacob.... When God comes to you, you shall carry up my bones from here" (Genesis 50:24–25).

After Jesus' death and resurrection, he promised to be with us always, even to the end of the world (see Matthew 28:20). There are no bones to be carried, as Mary Magdalene had thought, for he lives.

Dear Joseph, your promise has been fulfilled: God has indeed come to us, in the flesh, and he remains with us always.

FOR REFLECTION:

1. Who are the people in my life through whom the resurrected Christ reveals himself?

2. What experiences do I have of God's bringing good out of evil?

3. When have I received or given mercy in a close relationship? How has this mercy affected me, the other person and the relationship?

CHAPTER EIGHT

Moses and the People and Jesus in the Desert

Good plays favorites. There is no getting around it. God's method in entering history is always to choose a particular person in a particular way. Think of Abraham, Joseph and Moses. Jesus chose twelve apostles from among his disciples, and of those twelve, Peter, James and John were closer to him than the others.

The choice does not have to do with the person's strength or ability; it is simply God's choice. In fact, God frequently seems to choose a weak person in order to make it clear that it is God's power that saves and not that of the chosen person. Saint Paul was a persecutor of Christians before he was chosen. At a certain point he asked the Lord to take his weakness away, and the Lord responded, "My grace is sufficient for you, for power is made perfect in weakness" (2 Corinthians 12:9).

When I speak of this method of choice to my students, they normally become offended, which is understandable. A student named Ed once dared to articulate the reason God's "favoritism" is immediately offensive. "I don't like this because I want to be the favorite," he said. Isn't this true for all of us? Isn't this the reason Joseph's brothers were jealous of him?

Surely the desire to be loved by God in a particular way is a God-given desire. It is part of who we are. But there is a better way to respond to this desire than the way Joseph's brothers did.

If we make the effort to go past our immediate reactions, we will see that when God chooses one person over others, and when Jesus prefers certain disciples to others, it is never to exclude the others. Rather, his design is that through the chosen person others may also be chosen and experience God's preferential love.

Abraham's wife, his descendants and his tribe shared with him and through him in God's election. Joseph was chosen for the good of his brothers. Saint Paul was chosen so that he could become the most important missionary of the Church. As Paul and the other apostles must have felt preferred because they had met Jesus in the flesh, others would later feel preferred because they had met these apostles in the flesh.

Later in the Church's life, God chose Saint Francis; his followers, the Franciscans, must have felt particularly graced to have the privilege of being friends with him. Later still a friendship and a community grew up around Saint Ignatius. God chose Mother Teresa so that all of her sisters and all of the poor they served would experience God's preference for them.

My vocation to the priesthood came because God chose Monsignor Luigi Giussani, and I met those who had the opportunity to be friends with him in the Communion and Liberation Movement. I found my vocation verified in my friendship with Father Richard Neilson, a priest I happened to meet in New York. Had he not responded to God's call to him, I may not have become certain of God's call to me.

Marriage is joyful because one person has chosen you over all the other people he or she could have spent life with. The Church recognizes this preferential love as sacramental!

God loves us with a personal love, and therefore he must come to me through a person. I have named names in order to emphasize the particularity with which God enters our lives and chooses us. If I do not experience God's love in particular personal relationships with particular persons, then to hear that God loves me does not make much difference to me. It is simply a nice idea.

God is not generic, and he doesn't come to us generically. God prefers, God chooses, God calls, because God reveals himself as a Person, as a Father who has a personal affection for each of his children. The summit of this personal revelation is Jesus Christ, God and man.

GOD AND MOSES

In the Old Testament God's method of choosing and identifying himself with a particular person is clearly evident in the person of Moses. When God chooses Moses to go back to Egypt and free his people, Moses objects, "O my Lord, I have never been eloquent…. I am slow of speech and slow of tongue…. O my Lord, please send someone else" (see Exodus 4:10, 13).

Verse 14 tells us that the Lord becomes angry with Moses, because the Lord has promised to be with him and still Moses complains. Particularly heinous is Moses' asking God to send someone else, for God has made his choice.

With infinite patience God tells Moses that he will send Aaron along to speak for Moses; however, it is clear that Moses is the chosen one. For God tells Moses, "You shall serve as God for him" (Exodus 4:16). Yes, you read it right! Go look in the Bible and make sure! "You shall serve *as God for him!*" Once you look that up, as your mouth is still agape in shock, read a bit further, where God says to Moses, "See, I have made you like God to Pharaoh, and your brother Aaron shall be your prophet" (Exodus 7:1).

God has chosen Moses and is identifying himself with him. For Aaron and Pharaoh, and later for the Jewish people, to listen to God is to listen to Moses, and to follow God is to follow Moses.

We see this also in God's promise to save his people with his outstretched arm: "I am the LORD, and I will free you from the burdens of the Egyptians and deliver you from slavery to them. I will redeem you with an outstretched arm and with mighty acts of judgment…. The Egyptians shall know that I am the LORD, when I stretch out my hand against Egypt and bring the Israelites out from among them" (Exodus 6:6; 7:5).

Keeping in mind God's promise in the above verses, read what happens at the critical point of Israel's liberation. When the Israelites are encamped at the Red Sea and the Egyptians come in pursuit of them, God says to Moses, "But you lift up your staff, and stretch out your hand over the sea and divide it, that the Israelites may go into the sea on dry ground" (Exodus 14:16). And then, "Moses stretched out his hand over the sea. The LORD drove the sea back by a strong east wind all night, and turned the sea into dry land; and the waters were divided" (Exodus 14:21).

God promises the people that he will save them with his own hand. At the moment of salvation, it is Moses' out-stretched hand that is the saving hand of God. How blessed is Moses to be chosen to be God's method of saving his people! How blessed are those people chosen to witness God's saving action offered to them through Moses!

THE PASSOVER

We must not forget the reason the Israelites made it as far as the Red Sea in the first place, for God's chosen people remember and repeat it to this day, just as God's new chosen people remember and repeat the Mass.

The last plague visited upon the Egyptians was the death of every firstborn. In order to be saved from this plague of death, the Israelites had to procure an unblemished lamb, slaughter it, put its blood on their doorposts and eat its flesh. Seeing blood on a doorpost, the Lord would pass over that house, and the firstborn would be saved from the Lord's destructive blow.

The suffering, death and resurrection of Jesus, who celebrated Passover with his apostles, is seen as the fulfillment of Passover. Jesus is the unblemished Lamb, as John the Baptist pointed out to the first disciples (see John 1:29). It is the blood of Jesus, the Lamb of God, that delivers us from the death of sin. Passover is fulfilled in the Mass, because the flesh of the sacrificed, unblemished lamb had to be eaten (see Exodus 12:8), just as we eat the flesh of Christ in the Eucharist.

In Passover and in the Mass we see the importance of memory for Jews and Christians, which I mentioned in the Introduction. Recall that Jewish and Christian memory is the remembrance of an event that is present now. Every time the

Jews celebrate Passover, they celebrate the fact that they are free from the Egyptians now! When we celebrate Mass we follow the commandment of Jesus to his apostles at the Last Supper, "Do this in remembrance of me" (Luke 22:19; 1 Corinthians 11:24). We recall that Jesus and the salvation he brings are present now, in the flesh, in the Eucharist.

DOUBT IN THE DESERT

Initially freedom for the Israelites doesn't feel so good. The desert is not a pleasant place, and the difficulties of the present can easily make one forget about the promise of the future and the graces already received. The Israelites frequently complain to Moses and even look with nostalgia upon their slavery in Egypt.

Three days after crossing the Red Sea, the Israelites finally come upon water, but it is too bitter to drink. This has to be frustrating. When they complain to Moses, Moses appeals to God (Moses' greatness was always his dependence upon God). God points out a piece of wood to Moses. When Moses throws the wood into the water, the water becomes fresh. After this the Lord assures the people that if they listen to his voice, he will be their healer (see Exodus 15:22–26).

Later in the desert the Israelites grumble against Moses because they are afraid that the whole community will die of famine. This fear implies a doubt in God's providence. In fact, Moses and Aaron tell the people, "Your complaining is not against us but against the LORD" (Exodus 16:8).

God responds by giving the people manna, bread from heaven. The bread itself is an education to trust in God. The people must take only a daily portion except on the day before the Sabbath, when they will take a double portion.

Anything they try to store for themselves beyond their daily need will rot. At the conclusion of their journey, Moses will remind the people of the reason God kept them in the desert for forty years:

> Remember the long way that the LORD your God has led you these forty years in the wilderness, in order to humble you, testing you to know what was in your heart, whether or not you would keep his commandments. He humbled you by letting you hunger, then by feeding you with manna, with which neither you nor your ancestors were acquainted, in order to make you understand that one does not live by bread alone, but by every word that comes from the mouth of the LORD. (Deuteronomy 8:2–3)

God allowed the people to hunger in order that they might be educated to depend completely on him, to trust completely in him, to find their certainty in him.

The education didn't quite take. After the manna episode the Israelites again complain to Moses for the lack of water. Moses once again responds, "Why do you quarrel with me? Why do you test the LORD?" (Exodus 17:2). God instructs Moses to strike a rock, and water flows from it for the people to drink.

Later the Israelites complain not just about hunger and thirst but even about the quality of the food God is giving: "Why have you brought the assembly of the LORD into this wilderness for us and our livestock to die here? Why have you brought us up out of Egypt, to bring us to this wretched place? It is no place for grain, or figs, or vines, or pomegranates; and there is no water to drink" (Numbers 20:4–5).

This time God sends the people a reminder of the sinfulness of their complaints. This reminder comes in the form of deadly serpents. When the people repent, God instructs Moses to make a serpent and put it on a pole. When people who were bitten by a serpent look at the bronze serpent, they do not die. God fulfills his promise to be the people's healer if they trust him.

Signs of Jesus

One could choose to believe that the objects God used to answer the Israelites' complaints were chosen randomly, with no particular meaning. I choose otherwise. If you're with me, keep reading.

I don't think it is too much of a stretch to recognize each of these responses as pointing to Jesus. Two of them were used by Jesus himself as images that prefigured him. In John's Gospel Jesus says, "As Moses lifted up the serpent in the wilderness, so must the Son of man be lifted up, that whoever believes in him may have eternal life" (John 3:14–15). As looking upon the bronze serpent saved the Jews from death, believing in Jesus raised up on the cross and raised up by his Father will give us eternal life and save us from death. The piece of wood thrown into the water to make it sweet instead of bitter also seems to prefigure the cross.

Jesus refers to the manna from heaven in his discourse on the Bread of Life in chapter six of John's Gospel: "I am the bread of life. Your ancestors ate the manna in the wilderness, and they died. This is the bread that comes down from heaven, so that one may eat of it and not die" (John 6:48–50).

The rock from which the water flows is an interesting image. Countless times the Old Testament refers to God as a rock, especially in the Psalms. In this context the rock is an image of certainty, something eternal and unshakeable upon which I can depend. Jesus seems to use this imagery about himself when he says, "Everyone then who hears these words of mine and acts on them will be like a wise man who built his house on rock. The rain fell, the floods came, and the winds blew and beat on that house, but it did not fall, because it had been founded on rock" (Matthew 7:24–25).

Perhaps the water from the rock is an image of the water that came from Jesus' side on the cross. Tradition sees this stream of blood and water as a stream that feeds the Church with the sacraments: water representing baptism and blood representing the Eucharist. If you think that "water from the rock equals blood and water from Jesus" is too much of a stretch, you can at least appreciate the traditional view of the water and blood as an image of Christ being the New Adam and the Church being born from his side. So my bringing up this imagery will not be a total loss.

We see God's mercy in the fact that he answers the Israelites' complaints, their lack of trust in him, by responding to their immediate needs in ways they do not expect. When we recognize these responses as images of Jesus, we see that they are much more than immediate remedies. Each response carries within it the promise of an eternal remedy, the promise of someone greater than Moses who would one day come to the desert.

CERTAINTY IN THE DESERT

The forty days that Jesus spends in the desert clearly echo the forty years his people spent there. What is different about how Jesus lives that desert time?

The answer hearkens back to what we said in chapter three regarding original sin. The Israelites' repeated complaints showed the weakness of their faith and trust in God. Doubt seemed to gain more ground with every difficulty. But when Jesus was in the desert, his certainty in his Father's love was unshakeable.

Jesus in the desert somehow "undid" the doubts of the Jews in the desert. At the cross Jesus would definitively "undo" sin, which is the flowering of doubt. Before considering the strong connection between the desert and the cross (already prophesied by the wood and the lifted serpent), let us look at Jesus' certainty before the devil in the desert.

As stated before, doubt is the currency of the devil; so the devil begins two of his three temptations with the phrase "If you are the Son of God" (see Matthew 4:1–11; Luke 4:1–13). The devil knows that the foundation of any sin is doubt of God, and the core of sin is betrayal of the Father. Recall Joseph, who understood that the most sinful aspect of lying with Potiphar's wife would be the betrayal of Potiphar's authority so generously exercised over him and entrusted to him.

The one temptation that does not begin with the implied doubt of "if you are the Son of God" is a direct attack on Jesus' relationship with his Father. Matthew recounts,

> Again, the devil took him to a very high mountain and showed him all the kingdoms of the world and their splendor; and he said to him, "All these I will give you, if you will fall down and worship me." Jesus said to him, "Away with you, Satan! for it is written,
>
> 'Worship the Lord your God,
> and serve only him.'" (Matthew 4:8–10)

To understand the emptiness of this temptation, I think of an old picture of my brother. My family had been at Palisades Amusement Park, and it was time to go home. My brother did not want to go, and so he hid from my parents. His pouting face peeking from behind a garbage can has been immortalized in our family photo album. He cried all the way home in the car.

Now imagine that my brother had peeked out from behind that garbage can and not found our parents there. Imagine his finding himself alone at the amusement park. What had been a little boy's heaven one moment would have become a little boy's hell. For when a small child is lost in an amusement park without his mother or father, no rides or games or cotton candy mean anything to him. When a child is lost without parents in a toy store or a ball field, no toy and no sport will bring him peace. The child wants his mommy or daddy, and nothing else will do.

I have told this story to first-graders and asked them where my brother would be happier, alone at the amusement park or crying in the car. Every student in every first-grade class has answered without hesitation that my brother was happier in the car.

"But he's crying!" I protest to them.

"But he's with his mommy and daddy," they respond with certainty.

Jesus understood the emptiness of the devil's offer of all the magnificence of all the kingdoms in the world. For without his Father all that magnificence would mean nothing. Separated from the Father there is no peace—only emptiness, only nothingness. Unity with the Father is everything; it is a fullness that no evil can conquer or compromise.

As my brother was happier crying in the car because his parents were with him, Jesus shows that we can face even suffering and death when we are in union with the Father. Recall that Jesus told the women weeping for him on the way to Calvary to weep for themselves, not for him (see Luke 23:27–31). Jesus did not need their pity; rather he pitied them. He had certainty in his Father's love, and they did not.

Jesus withstands the devil's temptations because he never doubts his Father. He indeed is the rock in the desert whose living water quenches the dryness of our doubt. Luke tells us that at the end of the forty days, "when the devil had finished every test, he departed from him until an opportune time" (Luke 4:13). That opportune time would come with the Passion. There Jesus answers each of the devil's temptations.

JESUS' ANSWERS TO THE TEMPTATIONS

The devil's first temptation has to do with hunger. This is interesting because all of the Israelites' complaints had to do with hunger and thirst. The devil tells Jesus, "If you are the Son of God, command these stones to become loaves of bread" (Matthew 4:3).

Jesus responds to this temptation at the Last Supper, when he turns bread to God. He shows the devil that his imagination is quite puny. Stones to bread is a mere magic trick; Jesus instead feeds us with what we truly hunger for, his real and enduring presence: "Your ancestors ate the manna in the wilderness, and they died. This is the bread that comes down from heaven, so that one may eat of it and not die" (John 6:49–50).

The second temptation follows:

> If you are the Son of God, throw yourself down; for it is
>   written,
>   "He will command his angels concerning you,"
>   and "On their hands they will bear you up,
>   so that you will not dash your foot against a stone."
> (Matthew 4:6)

When Jesus is arrested, one of his disciples takes a sword and cuts off the ear of the high priest's slave. John tells us that this disciple was Peter. Recall that when Peter objected to the suffering and death Jesus said he would undergo, Jesus rebuked him: "Get behind me, Satan! You are a stumbling block to me; for you are setting your mind not on divine things but on human things" (Matthew 16:23).

Peter is once again thinking as men do, and notice Jesus' rebuke this time, "Put your sword back into its place; for all who take the sword will perish by the sword. Do you think that I cannot appeal to my Father, and he will at once send me more than twelve legions of angels?" (Matthew 26:52–53).

I sometimes think of this as a "Clint Eastwood moment" in the Passion. It seems as if Jesus utters his rebuke directly to Satan. In the desert Satan tempted Jesus to test his Father's promise to send angels. Here Jesus is once again in a position in which he could ask the Father for angels, but Jesus doesn't need to test the Father's love. "I am certain of the Father," Jesus seems to say. "You will never have an 'opportune time' with me, because my Father is always with me. I and the Father are one."

THE CRY FROM THE CROSS

How does Jesus respond to the third temptation, that he could have all the kingdoms of the world if he would just bow down and worship Satan?

From the cross Jesus cries out, "My God, my God, why have you forsaken me?" (Mark 15:34). Jesus' utterances from the cross were not random. The Church has a long tradition of reflecting on what we call "the seven last words." This particular word is the first line of Psalm 22. In the time of Jesus the psalms were not numbered but were known by their first line. This cry to God the Father takes on greater depth when we look at the full psalm, which Jesus could not have recited in his extreme agony.

The psalm begins with cries of suffering:

> All who see me mock at me;
>> they make mouths at me, they shake their heads. (verse 7)
>> …
> Do not be far from me,
>> for trouble is near
>> and there is no one to help. (verse 11)
>> …
> I am poured out like water,
>> and all my bones are out of joint;
> my heart is like wax;
>> it is melted within my breast;
> my mouth is dried up like a potsherd,
>> and my tongue sticks to my jaws;
>> you lay me in the dust of death. (verses 14–15)

Then the psalm suddenly changes its tone to one of glory, certainty and authority:

I will tell of your name to my brothers and sisters;
    in the midst of the congregation I will praise you:
You who fear the LORD, praise him!
    All you offspring of Jacob, glorify him;
    stand in awe of him, all you offspring of Israel!
For he did not despise or abhor
    the affliction of the afflicted;
he did not hide his face from me,
    but heard when I cried to him.
From you comes my praise in the great congregation;
    my vows I will pay before those who fear him.
The poor shall eat and be satisfied;
    those who seek him shall praise the LORD.
May your hearts live forever!
All the ends of the earth shall remember
    and turn to the LORD;
and all the families of the nations
    shall worship before him.
For dominion belongs to the LORD,
    and he rules over the nations. (verses 22–28)

In these verses we see Jesus' response to the devil's third temptation. The devil wants Jesus to bow before him in exchange for all the kingdoms of the world, but Jesus responds that this dominion is the Lord's, not the devil's: "All the ends of the earth shall remember and turn to the LORD; / and all the families of the nations shall worship before him."

In fact, this psalm is a beautiful synthesis of Jesus' undoing the Israelites' doubt in the desert and fulfilling the promises that were made there:

"The poor shall eat and be satisfied": the true hunger will be filled.

"May your hearts live forever": death will no longer threaten us or hold sway.

"I will tell of your name to my brothers and sisters; / in the midst of the congregation I will praise you: / You who fear the LORD, praise him! / all you offspring of Jacob, glorify him, / stand in awe of him, all you offspring of Israel!": Jesus is inviting Israel, his brothers, to doubt no longer but to stand before God in trust and awe at his faithfulness.

Jesus' death and resurrection are the ultimate reassurance that we need never doubt. Even on the cross Jesus proclaims his certainty. Here is where he undid the doubt of the desert and of all places and all times.

OBEDIENCE LEADS TO SALVATION

Recall that after the first complaint in the desert, God said to the Israelites, "If you will listen carefully to the voice of the LORD your God, and do what is right in his sight, and give heed to his commandments and keep all his statutes, I will not bring upon you any of the diseases that I brought upon the Egyptians; for I am the LORD who heals you" (Exodus 15:26).

But the Israelites could not listen carefully to the Lord. They could not do what was right, just as we cannot listen to the Lord and do what is right. God, in his fatherly mercy, has had pity on us poor wandering children. He sent his Son to wander through the same desert as the Israelites, to suffer the same temptations, difficulties and death of all humanity.

But his Son did it differently. He never doubted. He was the One who listened to the voice of the Lord. He is the only one who deserves to be spared all the plagues brought upon the Egyptians. But as Joseph shared his victory with his brothers, Jesus shares his victory with us, his brothers. He is truly the Lord who heals us.

Jesus is the one who fulfilled the covenant with Moses, as he is the one who fulfilled the covenant with Abraham.

FOR REFLECTION:

1. Do I recognize the desire to be chosen in my own experience?

2. Which is a deeper need of the human person: to be rewarded for our efforts and talents or to be chosen by one who loves us?

CHAPTER NINE

Return of the King

After the Israelites entered into the Promised Land, they lived through the period of the Judges. During this time they did not have a king like other nations, for the Lord was their king.

A judge was a man or woman called by God to lead the Israelites during a time of particular danger. Probably the most well-known judge is Samson, whose strength was taken away when his betrayer, Delilah, cut his hair off. In the final humiliating moments of his life, Samson brought the temple down upon his enemies, "so those he killed at his death were more than those he had killed during his life" (Judges 16:30).

The last judge of Israel was Samuel. When he became old he tried to pass on his judgeship to his sons, but they were corrupt, and nowhere does it say that the Lord was with them as he was with the other judges (see 1 Samuel 8:1–3). At this point the Israelites complained to Samuel, "You are old and your sons do not follow in your ways; appoint for us, then, a king to govern us, like other nations" (1 Samuel 8:5).

REQUEST AND REPERCUSSION

As soon as the Israelites ask to be like the other nations, something is wrong. They have forgotten who they are. For the Israelites are God's chosen people; they are supposed to be different from all the other nations as a witness to that fact. Moses told them, "For you are a people holy to the LORD your God; it is you the LORD has chosen out of all the peoples on earth to be his people, his treasured possession" (Deuteronomy 14:2).

The Israelites' request immediately displeases Samuel, but the Lord's response to Samuel's prayer in this moment is, "Listen to the voice of the people in all that they say to you; for they have not rejected you, but they have rejected me from being king over them" (1 Samuel 8:7). God hearkens to the request of the people, which is perhaps as amazing as Sarah's having a baby. Here is the all-powerful God, rejected by his own people, and he does not crush them but accedes to their request. He does not punish them but allows them to live through the dramatic consequences of their request.

And this request will usher in a drama that will play itself out over the subsequent thousand years and beyond into eternity. For aren't we all struggling with whether we want to trust God as our King or throw in our lot with someone or something else? Can't we all understand the Israelites' desire for a flesh-and-blood king they could see and touch?

The first chosen king is Saul, who is perhaps the most intolerable figure in the Bible. In Revelation Jesus issues a serious warning to some so-so Christians, "Because you are lukewarm, and neither cold nor hot, I am about to spit you out of my mouth" (Revelation 3:16). Saul is the patron of the lukewarm.

When Saul receives God's call to be king through Samuel, Saul is nowhere to be found. Everyone is looking around for him, until the Lord himself has to intervene and let them know he is hiding in the baggage. (I'm not kidding! Read 1 Samuel 10:17–27.) Saul's halfhearted yes continues throughout his kingship. He disobeys God's commands but tries to justify himself (see 1 Samuel 13:8–14); he awakens poor Samuel from the afterlife so he can whine to him (1 Samuel 28:3–15); he's jealous and moody (1 Samuel 16:14–23; 18:7–9, 28–29).

Let's not waste any more words on Saul. Let's move on. This is exactly what God did when he said, "I regret that I made Saul king" (1 Samuel 15:11).

THE PROMISE TO DAVID

Now that we have spewed out Saul, let us turn our eyes where God turned his, toward Bethlehem. God sent Samuel there to choose a king from among Jesse's sons. The one ultimately chosen was the least expected, for each of the elder sons seemed to Samuel fit to be king. The Lord corrected Samuel: "For the LORD does not see as mortals see; they look on the outward appearance, but the LORD looks on the heart" (1 Samuel 16:7).

The one son who had not come to the sacrifice to which Samuel had invited Jesse and his family was the youngest, David, for he was out in the fields shepherding the sheep. Samuel sent for him, and as David approached the Lord said to Samuel, "Rise and anoint him; for this is the one" (1 Samuel 16:12).

The Lord did not give David the kingship immediately, and David would not take it upon himself until the Lord gave it to him. He would be a great and admirable king. True, he would sin gravely, but he would never justify his evil actions; when confronted with his own sin, he always repented.

In a peaceful moment of his kingly reign, David decided that he would build a temple for the ark of the covenant. The Lord took offense at this: "Wherever I have moved about among all the people of Israel, did I ever speak a word with any of the tribal leaders of Israel, whom I commanded to shepherd my people Israel, saying, 'Why have you not built me a house of cedar?'" (2 Samuel 7:7). Who is David to build a house for God?

Recall the ritual of the covenant God made with Abraham. Abraham didn't walk through the animals; only God did. Recall that it was not Abraham who offered his son but God who offers his. Recall the responses to the Jews' complaints in the desert, which prophesy that Jesus would be the one to fulfill the covenant on Mount Sinai.

As God himself, through his Son, kept the covenant with Abraham and Moses, God will make and keep a covenant with David. In front of David's proud promise, the Lord responds that it is not David who will build a house for God but rather God who will build a house for David—through David's son.

> When your days are fulfilled and you lie down with your ancestors, I will raise up your offspring after you, who shall come forth from your body, and I will establish his kingdom. He shall build a house for my name, and I will establish the throne of his kingdom forever. I will be a father to him, and he shall be a son to me. When he commits iniquity, I will punish him with a rod such as mortals use, with blows inflicted by human beings. But I will not take my steadfast love from him, as I took it from Saul, whom I put away from before you. Your house and your kingdom shall be made sure forever before me; your throne shall be established forever. (2 Samuel 7:12–16)

God promises David that his kingdom will last forever. This promise will be repeated in the Psalms and recalled by the prophets. It will be associated ever after with David, for that king's greatness did not come from himself but from the promise the Lord made to him.

THE TEMPLE AND THE TEMPTATIONS OF SOLOMON AND HIS SUCCESSORS

The promise to David seems to be fulfilled immediately in his son Solomon. Solomon was the second son born to David and Bathsheba. (The first son died by God's design, because David had killed by design Bathsheba's husband, Uriah the Hittite, to cover up his adulterous affair with Bathsheba. You can read 2 Samuel 11 and 12 for the scandalous details and for an example of God's mercy and of David's humble repentance.)

With the materials that his father David had collected for the building of the temple, King Solomon set about having it built. When it was completed, the Lord visited Solomon and gave him a promise and a warning:

> I have consecrated this house that you have built, and put my name there forever; my eyes and my heart will be there for all time. As for you, if you will walk before me, as David your father walked, with integrity of heart and uprightness, doing according to all that I have commanded you, and keeping my statutes and my ordinances, then I will establish your royal throne over Israel forever, as I promised your father David, saying, "There shall not fail you a successor on the throne of Israel."
>
> If you turn aside from following me, you or your children, and do not keep my commandments and my statutes that I have set before you, but go and serve other gods and worship

them, then I will cut Israel off from the land that I have given them; and the house that I have consecrated for my name I will cast out of my sight; and Israel will become a proverb and a taunt among all peoples. This house will become a heap of ruins; everyone passing by it will be astonished, and will hiss; and they will say, "Why has the LORD done such a thing to this land and to this house?" (1 Kings 9:3–8)

Note that if Solomon and his successors turn from God's commandments, they will lose their land and the house they have built. However, mysteriously, God's name and his heart and his eyes will remain with that house forever.

As a result of his many foreign wives, Solomon did turn from the Lord to strange gods and did evil in the sight of the Lord. The Lord told Solomon that because of this the kingdom would be split into two under his son Rehoboam (see 1 Kings 11:1–13).

Rehoboam was a very unwise ruler, and the unrest and resentment he caused occasioned the splitting of the kingdom around 921 BC. There was the northern kingdom called Israel, with Samaria as its capital, and the southern kingdom, called Judah, with Jerusalem as its capital. For two hundred years the northern and the southern kingdoms suffered under many kings who did evil in the sight of the Lord.

In 721 BC the northern kingdom fell to the Assyrians, and the northern tribes disappeared from history. They had become so much like other nations as to be indistinguishable from them. Around 586 BC the southern kingdom fell to Babylon. The chosen people were exiled from their land, and their enemies had destroyed the temple, in accordance with

God's warning to Solomon. We will look more closely at the fall of these kingdoms in the next chapter.

EXILE

The period of exile must have been one of great confusion for God's chosen people. What about the promise made to David? Not only had the kingdom been divided, but both kingdoms had been definitively conquered. Had God broken his promise because of the sins of the kings and the people?

This doesn't seem to make sense when we think of God's faithfulness to Abraham and Sarah. It certainly does not make sense when we look at the unconditional promise to David: "Your house and your kingdom shall be made sure forever before me; your throne shall be established forever" (2 Samuel 7:16). And consider the repetition of this promise in God's warning to Solomon: "I have consecrated this house that you have built, and put my name there forever; my eyes and my heart will be there for all time" (1 Kings 9:3).

What a painful and persistent memory this promise must have been! We see that persistence among those Israelites who would not forget who they were. The challenge the Jews faced in remaining faithful to their God-given uniqueness and traditions in the cultural environment of Babylon must have been great. Perhaps those remaining faithful to Christianity today can understand their difficulty, especially those trying to pass the Christian faith on to their children in our secularized contemporary world.

Years later, under Cyrus, king of Persia, God's people were permitted to return to Jerusalem and rebuild the temple (as the Babylonians had destroyed the first one). To understand something of the greatness of the remnant who returned, let me offer an example.

If tomorrow someone were to come and tell me, "We've got it all set with visa and working papers; you can go back and live in Ireland," I am sure I would decline the offer. No offense to the country of Ireland, but I have never been there. My life is in the United States. Ireland was the home of some of my ancestors, not my home. (In order to be fair to both sets of my ancestors, let it be known that I would not move to Greece tomorrow either.)

Many of the Jews who left Babylon, somewhere around fifty years after the exile, had never been to Jerusalem. They had lived their lives in Babylon. So why did they go back?

Recall what has been said about Jewish (and Christian) memory. It is not merely looking to the past but recognizing a presence that began before you and that impacts your life here and now. That is, it is the mother saying to the child, "Remember who you're talking to!"

The remnant of Israel did not forget who they were; they did not forget their history, which only God's election could explain. They understood the origin and meaning of their prayers and practices, and they kept alive the awareness of God and of themselves toward which these gestures educated them. It is of this people that the prophet Isaiah wrote:

> Comfort, O comfort my people,
>   says your God.
> Speak tenderly to Jerusalem,
>   and cry to her
> that she has served her term,
>   that her penalty is paid,

that she has received from the LORD's hand
　　double for all her sins.
A voice cries out:
"In the wilderness prepare the way of the LORD,
　　make straight in the desert a highway for our God.
Every valley shall be lifted up,
　　and every mountain and hill be made low;
the uneven ground shall become level,
　　and the rough places a plain.
Then the glory of the LORD shall be revealed,
　　and all people shall see it together,
　　for the mouth of the LORD has spoken." (Isaiah 40:1–5)

What a debt we owe to this people whom Isaiah rightly calls "the glory of the LORD." They lived the memory of the Lord in Babylon to the point that they survived as a people, and now as they journeyed back from Babylon to Jerusalem, they had become the memory of the Lord. They were a physical and astounding reminder of his presence, unwitting prophets of his future and definitive coming into the world. They revealed the glory of the Lord as they returned to Jerusalem in faithfulness not to a promise they had made to the Lord but to a promise that the Lord had made to them.

The Hope of the Prophets

The Jews had indeed survived as a people, and God had been with them not only spiritually but in the persons and the words of the prophets who arose during the period of kings and continued during and after the exile. The words of the prophets were reminders that God is always faithful to his promises. Notice how these words serve as a kind of bridge between the promise to David and the coming of Christ:

But you, O Bethlehem of Ephrathah,
    who are one of the little clans of Judah,
from you shall come forth for me
    one who is to rule in Israel,
    whose origin is from of old, from ancient days.
(Micah 5:2, around 700 BC, emphasis added)

Hear then, *O house of David!* Is it too little for you to weary mortals, that you weary my God also? Therefore the Lord himself will give you a sign. Look, *the young woman is with child and shall bear a son, and shall name him Immanuel.*
(Isaiah 7:13–14, 740–700 BC, emphasis added)

The people who walked in darkness
    have seen a great light;
those who lived in a land of deep darkness—
    on them has light shined....
For a child has been born for us,
    a son given to us;
authority rests upon his shoulders;
    and he is named
Wonderful Counselor, Mighty God,
    Everlasting Father, Prince of Peace.
His authority shall grow continually,
    and there shall be endless peace
for the throne of David and his kingdom.
He will establish and uphold it
    with justice and with righteousness
from this time onwards and *forevermore.*
(Isaiah 9:2, 6–7, 740–700 BC, emphasis added)

The days are surely coming, says the LORD, when *I will raise up for David a righteous Branch,* and he shall reign as king and deal wisely, and shall execute justice and righteousness in the land.

In his days Judah will be saved and Israel will live in safety. And *this is the name by which he will be called: "The LORD is our righteousness."* (Jeremiah 23:5–6, 627–587 BC, emphasis added)

On that day the LORD will shield the inhabitants of Jerusalem *so that the feeblest among them on that day shall be like David, and the house of David shall be like God*, like the angel of the LORD, at their head. And on that day I will seek to destroy all the nations that come against Jerusalem.

And I will pour out a spirit of compassion and supplication on the house of David and the inhabitants of Jerusalem, *so that, when they look on the one whom they have pierced, they shall mourn for him, as one mourns for an only child*, and weep bitterly over him, as one weeps over a firstborn.
(Zechariah 12:8–10, 520 BC, emphasis added)

The Jews did not forget the promise made to David, although it must have been difficult to understand even after they rebuilt the temple and resettled the land. For while they were once again in their own land, they continued to be subject to other empires.

Five hundred years after the return from exile, the Jews were a small people and a small land within the vast Roman Empire. The promise to David must have seemed distant, just as the event of Christ's coming sadly seems peripheral to many Christians of our time.

THE RETURN OF THE KING

With God's promise to David, this brief history of the kings and these few prophecies in the forefront of our minds, let us now receive the announcements of the coming of Jesus with the expectant heart of God's faithful chosen people.

In the sixth month the angel Gabriel was sent by God to a town in Galilee called Nazareth, to a virgin engaged to a man whose name was Joseph, *of the house of David*. The virgin's name was Mary. And he came to her and said, "Greetings, favored one! The Lord is with you." But she was much perplexed by his words and pondered what sort of greeting this might be. The angel said to her, "Do not be afraid, Mary, for you have found favor with God. And now, you will conceive in your womb and bear a son, and you will name him Jesus. He will be great, and will be called the Son of the Most High, *and the Lord God will give to him the throne of his ancestor David. He will reign over the house of Jacob forever, and of his kingdom there will be no end*." (Luke 1:26–33, emphasis added)

An angel of the Lord appeared to him in a dream and said, *"Joseph, son of David*, do not be afraid to take Mary as your wife, for the child conceived in her is from the Holy Spirit. She will bear a son, and you are to name him Jesus, for he will save his people from their sins." (Matthew 1:20–21, emphasis added)

In that region there were *shepherds living in the fields*, keeping watch over their flock by night. Then an angel of the Lord stood before them, and the glory of the Lord shone around them, and they were terrified. But the angel said to them, "Do not be afraid; for see—I am bringing you good news of great joy for all the people: *to you is born this day in the city of David a Savior, who is the Messiah, the Lord*. This will be a sign for you: you will find a child wrapped in bands of cloth and lying in a manger." And suddenly there was with the angel a multitude of the heavenly host, praising God and saying,

"Glory to God in the highest heaven,
and on earth peace among those whom he favors!"

When the angels had left them and gone into heaven, the shepherds said to one another, *"Let us go now to Bethlehem* and

see this thing that has taken place, which the Lord has
made known to us." So they went with haste and found Mary
and Joseph, and the child lying in the manger.
(Luke 2:8–16, emphasis added)

The name David carries with it the weight and the hope of
God's promise. The king whose kingdom will last forever is
to come from the lineage of David, just as the king who would
build a house for the Lord was to come from the lineage of
David. Thus it is important that Luke and Matthew reveal to
us that Joseph is of the house of David. For although he is
the adoptive father of Jesus, Jesus will be considered a part of
his house.

It is important that Jesus is born in Bethlehem, the city of
David, God's anointed king. Luke further emphasizes that
the first announcement of the birth of Jesus was made to
shepherds in the fields around Bethlehem. Why not carpenters? Why not rabbis? Because David was a shepherd in the
fields around Bethlehem!

So important is the promise made to David for an understanding of the identity of Jesus, that when two blind men call
out to Jesus, "Lord, have mercy on us, Son of David," while
the crowd is yelling at them to be quiet, Jesus calls them to
himself and asks them what they want him to do for them
(see Matthew 20:29–34). These men may be physically blind,
but their perception of Jesus' identity is keener than that of
the rest of the crowd. Perhaps Jesus calls them to himself
because he appreciates their faith in him as the eternal king,
the promise fulfilled.

For it is not Solomon but Jesus who is the righteous branch
of David, who will reign and deal wisely as prophesied by

Jeremiah. It is Jesus who will build the everlasting house of the Lord.

In fact, Jesus *is* the everlasting temple of the Lord. He speaks of himself in this way in John's Gospel: "Jesus answered them, 'Destroy this temple, and in three days I will raise it up.' The Jews then said, 'This temple has been under construction for forty-six years, and will you raise it up in three days?' But he was speaking of the temple of his body" (John 2:19–21).

We ourselves are living stones built into that house (see 1 Peter 2:5). This fact helps us understand the prophecy of Zechariah that "the house of David shall be like God" (Zechariah 12:8). What could this mean? How is this possible? Because Jesus is God, and he continues his presence in the world through his Church, which is his mystical body, the mysterious yet real continuation of the body of Christ. The Church is the living house, the living body that Jesus has built, and so the house of David is like God!

Note also that Zechariah prophesies not only the coming of Jesus into the world but also his death when he says, "When they look on the one whom they have pierced, they shall mourn for him, as one mourns for an only child, and weep bitterly over him, as one weeps over a firstborn" (Zechariah 12:10). Surely Pontius Pilate had no idea that he was a prophet and evangelist when he ordered the inscription on Jesus' cross, "Jesus of Nazareth, the King of the Jews," *Iesus Nazarenus, Rex Iudaeorum* (John 19:19; see Matthew 27:37; Mark 15:26).

THE EXPECTED AND UNIMAGINED RETURN OF GOD

To fully appreciate what has happened in this marvelous history, we must go back even before God made the promise to David. For David was promised a king, but in Jesus we have more than a king.

Recall that when the Jews asked Samuel for a king, God informed Samuel that they were rejecting God as their king. They wanted a human king rather than their divine one. Now God has given them everything, for in Jesus they have a king who is human *and* divine. God is once again their king, because God has become the human king they asked for.

Consider some of the facts we have looked at so far:

- Sarah lied to God, and God honored his promise to Sarah.

- Abraham did not sacrifice his son to God, but God would sacrifice his only son for Abraham and his descendants.

- The Jews complained to God in the desert after God had saved them from Egypt, and God promised them a Savior.

- David promised to build God a house, and God built a house for David.

- The Jews chose a human king over God, and God became the human king they asked for.

We have reason to laugh and rejoice with Sarah and with Abraham and Moses and David.

FOR REFLECTION:

1. Can I point to stories in history and in my personal history in which God has written straight with crooked lines, as he did in the history of the kings?

2. How does this history make a difference in how I face difficult and confusing moments in life?

3. Am I certain that God is at work even in these difficult moments?

CHAPTER TEN

The Samaritan and the King

In this chapter we will take a closer look at the fall of the northern and southern kingdoms and how this sheds light on one of the most well-known of Jesus' parables.

THE FALL OF ISRAEL, THE SHAME OF THE SAMARITANS

In about the year 721 BC the kingdom of Israel, whose capital was Samaria, fell to the king of Assyria. After conquering a land, the Assyrians would deport most of its population to various parts of the Assyrian Empire. Second Kings tells us:

> In the fourth year of King Hezekiah, which was the seventh year of King Hoshea son of Elah of Israel, King Shalmaneser of Assyria came up against Samaria, besieged it, and at the end of three years, took it. In the sixth year of Hezekiah, which was the ninth year of King Hoshea of Israel, Samaria was taken. The king of Assyria carried the Israelites away to Assyria, settled them in Halah, on the Habor, the river of Gozan, and in the cities of the Medes, because they did not obey the voice of the LORD their God but transgressed his covenant—all that Moses the servant of the LORD had commanded; they neither listened nor obeyed. (2 Kings 18:9–12)

Some Jews would have been left in Samaria, and these eventually would intermingle with various other peoples whom Assyria would have sent to occupy the land. The Samaritans who descended from this intermingling would have a mix of Jewish and gentile blood.

The fall of the northern kingdom was seen as a judgment of God upon the northern Israelites. In fact, the first northern king, Jeroboam, had created his own shrines so that his people would not go down and worship in Jerusalem:

> Then Jeroboam said to himself, "Now the kingdom may well revert to the house of David. If this people continues to go up to offer sacrifices in the house of the LORD at Jerusalem, the heart of this people will turn again to their master, King Rehoboam of Judah; they will kill me and return to King Rehoboam of Judah." So the king took counsel, and made two calves of gold. He said to the people, "You have gone up to Jerusalem long enough. Here are your gods, O Israel, who brought you up out of the land of Egypt." He set one in Bethel, and the other he put in Dan. And this thing became a sin, for the people went to worship before the one at Bethel and before the other as far as Dan. (1 Kings 12:26–30)

When the Jews returned to Jerusalem to rebuild the temple, they refused the help the Samaritans offered. This may have been because of the Samaritans' mixed blood, because of their historic turning away from Jerusalem or because their fate seemed to be an even worse judgment of God than had the Babylonian subjugation of the southern kingdom. For the great majority of the northern tribes were deported and never heard from again, becoming what are known as the lost tribes of Israel.

What could be more shameful to a Jew than forgetting

your identity as God's chosen people? Hostility toward the Samaritans lasted down to the time of Jesus.

THE FALL OF JUDAH, THE SHAME OF THE JEWS

The kingdom of Judah must have found its fall utterly shameful, insulting and confusing. This southern kingdom had lasted more than a hundred years longer than the northern kingdom. The fall of the north was understandable. The north had built its own shrines with golden calves instead of worshiping in Jerusalem. Also, the north could not trace itself back to David as could the south. The split of the kingdom was an evil allowed by the Lord, but as long as the throne existed in Jerusalem, the promise made to David seemed intact.

So imagine how the fall of Judah and the retelling of it would wound the hearts of the chosen people.

> And in the ninth year of his reign, in the tenth month, on the tenth day of the month, King Nebuchadnezzar of Babylon came with all his army against Jerusalem, and laid siege to it; they built siegeworks against it all round. So the city was besieged until the eleventh year of King Zedekiah. On the ninth day of the fourth month the famine became so severe in the city that there was no food for the people of the land. Then a breach was made in the city wall; the king with all the soldiers fled by night by the way of the gate between the two walls, by the king's garden, though the Chaldeans were all around the city. They went in the direction of the Arabah. But the army of the Chaldeans pursued the king, and overtook him in the plains of Jericho; all his army was scattered, deserting him. Then they captured the king and brought him up to the king of Babylon at Riblah, who passed sentence on him.

> They slaughtered the sons of Zedekiah before his eyes, then put out the eyes of Zedekiah; they bound him in fetters and took him to Babylon. (2 Kings 25:1–7)

The slaying of Zedekiah's sons would seem to be the final insult, the shutting of the lid on the tomb of the promise made to David. For how can a kingdom go on when the king's sons have been killed?

OPEN WOUNDS

Many of us have painful events in our family histories or our personal histories that are rarely, if ever, mentioned. If they must be brought up, it is only with the greatest tact and tenderness. To mention the events casually is to irritate a wound.

Nations and peoples also bear such painful memories. We Americans can think of the wounds we bear from the attack on Pearl Harbor and those from the attack of September 11, 2001. Zedekiah's capture as he went from Jerusalem to Jericho would have been such an event for the Jewish people.

With this in mind, let us consider with new eyes and ears the parable Jesus tells about the Good Samaritan:

> "A man was going down from Jerusalem to Jericho, and fell into the hands of robbers, who stripped him, beat him, and went away, leaving him half dead. Now by chance a priest was going down that road; and when he saw him, he passed by on the other side. So likewise a Levite, when he came to the place and saw him, passed by on the other side. But a Samaritan while traveling came near him; and when he saw him, he was moved with pity. He went to him and bandaged his wounds, having poured oil and wine on them. Then he put him on his own animal, brought him to an inn, and took care of him. The next day he took out two denarii, gave them to the innkeeper,

and said, 'Take care of him; and when I come back, I will repay you whatever more you spend.' Which of these three, do you think, was a neighbor to the man who fell into the hands of the robbers?" He said, "The one who showed him mercy." Jesus said to him, "Go and do likewise." (Luke 10:29–37)

Would it be possible for the Jews of Jesus' time to hear about a man going from Jerusalem to Jericho who was overtaken by robbers without thinking of Zedekiah, the last king on the throne of David? For Zedekiah had escaped from Jerusalem and was overtaken and captured by the Chaldean soldiers in the plains of Jericho. Jesus seems to be taking a stab at Jewish pride. He seems to be speaking openly about a deep Jewish wound.

This is not unlike the way he spoke to the Samaritan woman at the well. Her deepest shame was that she had had five husbands and was living now with a man who was not her husband. When she said, "I have no husband," Jesus replied, "You are right in saying, 'I have no husband'; for you have had five husbands, and the one you have now is not your husband. What you have said is true!" (John 4:17–18).

Jesus had to know how much this would hurt the woman, and yet he said it. He said it because he loved her deeply. Had he not let her know that he knew about her shame, she would have walked away from that well thinking, "Well, he seems to like me, but if he really knew about me…"

Jesus penetrated to the painful depths of her heart because without that, nothing he would have said to her could have penetrated at all. The words would seem like the words of a man who really didn't know her. Instead Jesus showed that he was very familiar with her and with her shame, and knowing all of it, he still loved her. Jesus showed the Samaritan woman that her hope for love, which seemed irredeemably lost, was restored in him.

In the Bible seven is the perfect number. It is a symbol of perfection, fulfillment and rest. God rested and enjoyed his creation on the seventh day. Six, on the other hand, is a symbol of imperfection. The Samaritan woman had five husbands, and the sixth was less than a husband.

Jesus was number seven in this woman's life! Jesus was the fulfillment of what she had been looking for all the time. What she had perhaps given up hope of ever finding had become present, and his love for her was not only greater than what she had imagined but also completely different from her idea of how she would be loved.

THE GOOD SAMARITAN

With the parable of the Good Samaritan, Jesus may be opening a Jewish wound in order to show that he is the one who heals the wound, who answers the waning hope in a way greater than ever imagined. For the man going from Jerusalem to Jericho was the last vestige of the kingdom. He was left on the road half dead. Who can explain this tragedy? Who can proclaim the promise made to David and make sense of the history of salvation in the face of this event?

The priest and the Levite cannot. They go to the other side of the road, avoiding the pain and the seeming contradiction. A Samaritan comes along and does not look away but mercifully binds up the wounds of the half-dead man. Who is this Samaritan?

Let us peek back into John's Gospel, where some Jews accuse Jesus of being a Samaritan: "Are we not right in saying that you are a Samaritan and have a demon?" (John 8:48). Perhaps for the Jews, *Samaritan* was simply a generic word of insult, so much did they despise those people. This accusation occurred after Jesus very happily had called to himself the Samaritan woman and, through her, all the Samaritans in the nearby town.

Let us also note that Jesus did come from Nazareth, which was north of Samaria, in the territory that had belonged to the northern kingdom. If you look at Matthew's genealogy of Jesus, you will see that there were gentile women in the ancestral lineage of Jesus, so he was no stranger to mixed blood.

Whatever the reasons for the accusation, Jesus' response seems to indicate that he had no problem being spoken of as a Samaritan: "I do not have a demon; but I honor my Father, and you dishonor me" (John 8:49). He denied having a demon, but he did not find it necessary to deny the title "Samaritan," whatever was meant by it.

I would propose that the Samaritan in the parable is an image of Jesus. He can speak frankly about the fall of the kingdom, because he does not see it as an irredeemable tragedy. He, and only he, is the one who can bind up the wounds of the broken kingdom. He restores the kingdom and fulfills the promise made to David in a way that shatters expectations. He is not the kind of king the Jews were looking for, and his kingdom is not the limited political kingdom that they might have imagined; it is something eternally greater.

One of my students, Michael, pointed out in class that the innkeeper would seem then to be a disciple or perhaps even the Church. For the wounded man is entrusted to the innkeeper until the Samaritan comes back, as the kingdom is entrusted to us as we await the second coming of Christ.

A KINGDOM REDEEMED AND RESTORED

I once was giving a presentation with a Jewish rabbi for a campus ministry, when a college student asked the rabbi rather tactlessly whether Psalm 22 referred to Jesus. While I regretted the manner in which the question was posed, I was quite moved by the rabbi's response: "The Jews are not a spiritual people. If you want to free me, you can't give me spiritual freedom. I need freedom that is down-to-earth, here and now. Jesus came and went, and the Jews were still oppressed under Roman rule. He's not my messiah."

What a beautiful description of the Jewish people! God entered history, and so the Jew must see him active in history, here on earth, here and now!

At the same time, what can be more down-to-earth and less "spiritual" than God becoming human, the Word becoming flesh? Let us pray that we, the Church, come more and more into communion with Christ so that the freedom Jesus brings becomes as palpable and down-to-earth as possible, something that can be seen and touched here and now, in our very flesh. This is what the Church claims to be. This is what men and women of flesh and blood need the Church to be. The kingdom of God must be recognizable here and now. Let us, the heirs of the promise made to David, pray for the continual fulfillment of Zechariah's prophecy: "And the house of David shall be like God" (Zechariah 12:8).

FOR REFLECTION:

1. Has anyone in my life ever cut me to the heart as Jesus did the Samaritan woman and the Jews who listened to the parable of the Good Samaritan?

2. Are there friendships I recognize and respect as true even when they cause hurt?

3. How does the encounter of Jesus and the Samaritan woman help me better appreciate the importance of the sacrament of confession?

CHAPTER ELEVEN

Elijah and Elisha and the Ascension

In chapter six we spoke about some strange men who mysteriously appear in the Old Testament. In this chapter we will look at two strange men who mysteriously appear in the New Testament, and we will try to figure out who they might be and what their presence might mean. We will look at two other Old Testament figures for clues.

In the Acts of the Apostles, Luke tells us about the day of Jesus' ascension into heaven. Did you ever wonder why we celebrate the Ascension? It seems like a terribly sad day. The apostles watched Jesus physically disappear into the clouds. Were they crying? Did they have lumps in their throats? This is the man who had changed their lives, who had changed everything for them, and they would no longer see him as they had. It must have been hard to imagine how he would still be present with them. It must have been difficult to understand what his words meant, "It is to your advantage that I go away" (John 16:7).

Jesus also had spoken of a Counselor or a Paraclete whom he would send to them if he went away. Who was this Counselor? On the day of the Ascension itself, Jesus said, "You will receive power when the Holy Spirit has come upon you; and you will be my witnesses in Jerusalem, in all Judea and Samaria, and to the ends of the earth" (Acts 1:8)

Once Jesus said this, he was lifted up, and a cloud took him out of the apostles' sight. It is at this point that Luke tells us, "While he was going and they were gazing up towards heaven, suddenly two men in white robes stood by them. They said, 'Men of Galilee, why do you stand looking up toward heaven?'" (Acts 1:10–11).

Who were these robed men? Why don't they mind their own business? We are not told that the apostles even answered them. Could they have answered them? Did the apostles have a good reason to be staring into the sky even after Jesus had ascended?

Luke does not give us an answer to the question of the two men; he just leaves us with this bewildering scene. We turn to two men of the Old Testament who might help us unveil the mystery of this strange scene or at least appreciate its depth.

ELIJAH THE PROPHET AND ELISHA THE PLOWMAN

Elijah was a prophet from the north before the fall of the northern kingdom, and Elisha was his follower. You can read about Elijah in 1 Kings 17 through 2 Kings 2. He performed great miracles in Israel. He kept a widow and her son alive by assuring them that their near-empty jars of flour and oil would not run out during a drought he himself had predicted. He raised a dead boy to life. His prayers could call down fire and bring rain from heaven (see 1 Kings 17:1, 8–24; 18:20–46).

One day Elijah called Elisha to follow him. (Certainly writing and teaching about these two would have been easier had

Elijah called a disciple whose name was not so similar to his own. But God told Elijah whom to choose, and God chooses whom he wills.)

When he was called by Elijah, Elisha was a regular guy minding his own business, which was plowing with twelve yoke of oxen. Even more dramatic than the fishermen who would later leave their boats to follow Jesus, Elisha burned his plowing equipment in order to boil his twelve oxen for his family, and then he left everything to follow Elijah.

Elijah would continue his prophetic ministry, standing up fearlessly to the notorious King Ahab and later prophesying the death of that king's idolatrous son and successor, King Ahaziah. Ahaziah's captains and soldiers greatly feared Elijah, for they knew he could call fire down from heaven to destroy them.

Toward the end of his ministry, Elijah understood that he was to be taken up by God into heaven. You will find the story in 2 Kings 2. Elijah told Elisha that he was going on to Bethel, and he wanted Elisha to stay where he was. Elisha, who loved Elijah greatly, told him, "As the LORD lives, and as you yourself live, I will not leave you" (2 Kings 2:2).

Elisha then followed Elijah. When they arrived at Bethel, it seemed that news of Elijah's pending departure had leaked to the prophetic world. The guild prophets of Bethel asked Elisha, "Do you know that today the LORD will take your master away from you?" And Elisha replied, "Yes, I know; keep silent" (2 Kings 2:3).

Had Elisha lived in a later time on a different continent and spoken a different language, he may have said, "Shut up!" It seems Elisha too had some inkling of what was going to happen, and he did not like it.

Twice more Elijah told Elisha he was moving on, first to Jericho and then to the Jordan. Twice more he told Elisha to remain, and twice more Elisha vowed that he would not leave his master. The Jericho guild prophets, by the way, also could not resist revealing to Elisha that they were in the know, and they received the same curt response given to their Bethel comrades (see 2 Kings 2:5).

When Elijah and Elisha reached the Jordan, Elijah rolled up his mantel and struck the water, which promptly divided. When the two had crossed over, Elijah turned to his faithful disciple and said, "Tell me what I may do for you before I am taken from you" (2 Kings 2:9).

What did Elisha ask for? "Please," he said, "let me inherit a double share of your spirit."

Elisha may not have been a prophet yet, but his request for the spirit of Elijah shows his great intelligence and his great humanity. Elijah was a great prophet who had raised people from the dead and stood up to kings. Elisha, on the other hand, was a plowman, an ordinary farmer. How was he to carry on after Elijah? Merely repeating Elijah's words or telling stories about the great prophet would not change anything. Elisha knew that he and the Israelites needed the power and the presence of Elijah to continue among them.

We see Elisha's greatness in his simplicity and trust in Elijah and in God, which gave him the confidence to ask for what Elijah called "a hard thing." Elijah went on to tell Elisha, "If you see me as I am being taken from you, it will be granted you, if not, it will not" (2 Kings 2:10). At that moment a chariot of fire came between the two men and took Elijah up to heaven.

Elijah's ascension was accompanied by the dramatic cry of Elisha, "Father, father! The chariots of Israel and its horsemen!" (2 Kings 2:12). This cry is telling, for Elijah had become a father to Elisha; seeing him taken away could not have been easy. In obedience to Elijah and in longing for his presence, Elisha remained looking until he could see Elijah no more.

ELISHA THE PROPHET

Elisha apparently did not feel any different once Elijah disappeared into the heavens. In fact, he seems to have felt worse, for he tore his garment in two. He then picked up Elijah's mantle and began to walk home.

When I explain this story to young children, I speak about how sad and dejected Elisha must have been at this moment. The mantel must have been a very small consolation, like those T-shirts that say, "My parents went to ____, and all I got was this stupid T-shirt."

Elisha came up against the Jordan River. This must have been a particularly difficult moment. Not only was Elijah gone, but Elisha couldn't even get home. At this point he cried out, "Where is the LORD, the God of Elijah?" (2 Kings 2:14).

Elisha's cry echoes in the human heart as it confronts loss and tragedy: "Where is God?" This is, in fact, the cry of every human heart that takes life seriously. Without this cry no response by God will ever be recognized; for how can I recognize the answer when I haven't asked the question?

Elisha took the mantel and slammed it against the water. Was this a gesture of anger? Was it a gesture of faith?

Whatever was behind the gesture, God answered Elisha's cry and divided the water in two.

Where is God? He is with Elisha in the same way he was with Elijah!

The guild prophets of Jericho did not predict this. But they recognized what had happened when they saw Elisha: "The spirit of Elijah rests on Elisha," they said (2 Kings 2:15). Elisha's prayer was answered, and the presence of Elijah continued in Israel through Elisha.

Elisha would go on to perform great signs and wonders in Israel. Similar to Elijah, he saved a widow and her children by multiplying oil, and he raised a boy from the dead. Elisha would also multiply bread and cure Naaman the leper (see 2 Kings 4—5).

Elisha looked up into the sky as Elijah was taken up, and thus a plowman became a prophet. The disciple received his master's spirit and thus carried the very presence and power of his master.

THE APOSTLES AND THE PROPHETS: WAITING FOR THE SPIRIT

Now let us turn to the apostles, who are looking up into the sky as Jesus is taken up, and at those two robed men who ask them, "Why do you stand looking up toward heaven?"

The apostles' gaze at the ascension of Jesus is explained by Elisha's gaze at the ascension of Elijah. The apostles are looking up for the same reason Elisha was looking up: they want to receive the spirit of their master. Jesus promised, "You will be baptized with the Holy Spirit not many days from now" (Acts 1:5).

As Elisha the plowman could not have carried on the ministry of Elijah the prophet, these fishermen and tax collectors cannot carry the presence of Jesus into the world and into history by merely repeating Jesus' words and telling stories about him. The Church does not claim merely to pass on the message of Jesus but rather to be the continuation of his presence in the world through the gift of the Holy Spirit. As Elisha performed miracles similar to those of Elijah, we can see in the Acts of the Apostles how Jesus' disciples mysteriously carry on his very Person and presence after receiving the Holy Spirit he promised.

Peter encounters a crippled man at the temple gate and tells him, "I have no silver or gold, but what I have I give you; in the name of Jesus Christ of Nazareth, stand up and walk" (Acts 3:6). The man is healed and walks, just as those who were healed by Jesus did. Peter then speaks boldly and with authority to the people, just as Jesus did. After the healing and the speech, Peter and John are brought before the Sanhedrin and the high priest, just as Jesus was.

Acts 4:8 tells us that at this point Peter is "filled with the Holy Spirit." Peter and John are unafraid before the Sanhedrin, as Jesus was. In fact, we are told in Acts that when the rulers, elders and scribes "saw the boldness of Peter and John and realized that they were uneducated and ordinary men, they were amazed and recognized them as companions of Jesus" (Acts 4:13). Somehow their interrogators recognize the presence of Jesus in Peter and John.

Stephen, the first martyr, is another man who, we are told, is "filled with the Holy Spirit" (Acts 7:55). As he is being stoned to death, his own words echo the words uttered by Jesus on the cross. Jesus cried to the Father, "Father, into your hands I commend my spirit" (Luke 23:46), and Stephen cries to Jesus, "Lord Jesus, receive my spirit" (Acts 7:59). Jesus cried to the Father, "Father, forgive them; for they do not know what they are doing" (Luke 23:34). Stephen cries to Jesus, "Lord, do not hold this sin against them" (Acts 7:60).

It is interesting to note that in John's Gospel, when Jesus breathes the Holy Spirit upon the apostles, he tells them, "As the Father has sent me, so I send you" (John 20:21). As Jesus prays to the Father, so Stephen prays to Jesus.

The Spirit tells Philip to meet up with a chariot of an Ethiopian eunuch on his way from Jerusalem. Philip explains the Scriptures to the eunuch and, at the eunuch's request, baptizes him. Philip then disappears from sight (see Acts 8:26–40). This is exactly what the risen Christ did for the disciples who were leaving Jerusalem for Emmaus. He explained the Scripture to them, he performed a sacrament—in this case the Eucharist—and he disappeared from sight (see Luke 24:13–31).

The prophets of Jericho recognized that the spirit of Elijah rested on Elisha because Elisha did the same things as Elijah had done. Can we not recognize in these accounts of the early disciples that the spirit of Jesus, the Holy Spirit, came to rest upon his disciples? More importantly, I want to be able to say with certainty that the Spirit rests upon the Church, the mystical body of Christ, here and now.

THE HOLY SPIRIT

We cannot see the wind, but we know it is there because we can feel it and sometimes hear it and sometimes see dust or leaves carried by it or tree branches blown around by it. We cannot see the Holy Spirit, but we know that the Spirit is present through things we are able to see and touch.

Indeed, the Holy Spirit always makes Jesus present in ways we can see and touch. This happened first in the womb of Mary. The Holy Spirit came upon her, and thus Jesus became physically present in her womb.

This happens in the Eucharist when the priest asks that the Holy Spirit come upon the gifts of bread and wine, "that they may become the body and blood of Our Lord Jesus Christ."[1] Indeed, we invoke the Holy Spirit in every one of the sacraments. And what are the sacraments but the grace of Jesus Christ made visibly and tangibly present?

This happens in the Church, as we see in the Acts of the Apostles and throughout the history of the Church. The saints and all the faithful disciples of Jesus carry on his presence in a mysterious way. As we have already seen, when Jesus first appeared to Paul, he asked him, "Saul, Saul, why do you persecute me?" (Acts 9:4). Jesus did not refer to his followers as "them" but as "me." When Paul asked him who he was, Jesus emphasized his identity with his people with the answer, "I am Jesus, whom you are persecuting" (Acts 9:5).

Once we have received his Spirit, we become members of Christ's body. More than "new Elijahs," we become "other Christs."

In John's Gospel Jesus tells us, "Very truly, I tell you, the one who believes in me will also do the works that I do and, in fact, will do greater works than these" (John 14:12). Why greater? Because when the great prophet raises a boy from the dead, it seems in accord with his role as a great prophet; when the plowman does it, it is even more amazing. When the Son of God cures the cripple and stands fearless before the

Sanhedrin it is one thing, but when ordinary fishermen do the same, it is even more amazing.

If two thousand years after the fact, there are people who love Jesus because they have experienced his presence in the Church, then that means that for two thousand years he has shown himself through sinner after sinner after sinner. In his book *Why the Church?* Monsignor Giussani uses the image of gold in the mud to describe the presence of Christ in the members of his Church. The mud is undeniable, but for those who seek with desire and sincerity, the gold is just as undeniable. The gold is made present through the gift of the Holy Spirit.[2]

GOD IS WITH US

I will never forget a high school freshman class in which a young man named Anthony grew frustrated with me and said, "Father, if Jesus is present, where is he?"

I replied that Jesus is present among us.

"Which seat is he sitting in?" Anthony asked.

This was clearly a situation in which I needed the Holy Spirit to speak through me. A classroom of fourteen-year-old boys asking tough questions can be just as daunting as the kings and governors that Jesus warned us about (see Mark 13:9–11), especially when their questions are serious and you understand that their lives are infinitely important.

I told Anthony that often when certain students in the class said things or asked questions, I perceived that Jesus was working through them, whether by revealing something new about the Scripture we were studying or by showing me in what direction to take that particular class.

At that point another student chimed in, "Name names!"

I was moved by this request for particularity, and I did name names and quote quotes from our class that year. Many of the named boys seemed truly captivated and curious, much more so than if I were merely praising their good personal qualities. For it is truly amazing to contemplate that you, in all your ordinariness and sin and weakness, can be the very presence of Christ. This is the power of the Holy Spirit at work in the mystical body of Christ.

Anthony had asked the same question as Elisha the plowman, "Where is God?" The answer that Elijah and Elisha and the apostles longed for, and that Anthony and I and all the members of the Church have been given in our baptism through the grace of the Holy Spirit, is not a word but a Person: Jesus Christ, Emmanuel, "God is with us."

FOR REFLECTION:

1. When have I cried out, as Elisha did, "Where is God?"

2. Has an answer come to this cry?

3. Why did the apostles need the Spirit of Jesus? Could words alone have generated the Church?

CHAPTER TWELVE

Mary of Israel: Through Her the Old Is Made New

The unity of the Old and New Testaments is paradoxical. In the previous chapters we have seen how the New Testament takes on greater meaning when we look at the Old Testament; we have seen how the Old Testament seems to look forward to and long for the fulfillment brought about in Jesus Christ. However, while recognizing a continuity, we can never reduce the coming of Jesus Christ to an automatic or necessary outcome of the Old Testament. We must never forget the newness of the New Testament.

Luigi Giussani, John Paul II and Benedict XVI have all said, "Christianity is an event."[1] As much as the event of the Incarnation is in utter harmony with the longings of the Old Testament, it is also utterly beyond any human imagining or conjecture; it is a free act of God's unfathomable love. No amount of reading of the Old Testament would indicate to the reader that God himself would become human. The Word became flesh through the ever surprising and ever new grace of God, not as the result of a prophetic equation. It is only after the event of the incarnation, passion, death, resurrection and ascension of Jesus of Nazareth that we can recognize this event mysteriously embedded in the Hebrew Scriptures.

When Jesus appeared to the disciples after his resurrection, for instance, "he opened their minds to understand the scriptures" (Luke 24:45). Just hours before that he encountered the two discouraged disciples on the road to Emmaus, and "beginning with Moses and all the prophets, he interpreted to them the things about himself in all the scriptures" (Luke 24:27). We cannot be too hard in our judgment of those sad disciples, for how could they understand the mystery of the Scriptures before they experienced that mystery in the risen flesh?

We cannot express by words alone the paradox of Jesus' being a complete surprise and at the same time a complete fulfillment. For we are not speaking of poetry but of a Person; we are not concerned with ideas but with an individual, Jesus of Nazareth.

The old becomes new when the Word becomes flesh, and this happens in Mary.

THE NEW AND TRUE ARK OF THE COVENANT

We see the unity of surprise and fulfillment clearly in Mary's yes. The announcement of the angel is a complete surprise. "How can this be?" asks the Blessed Virgin.

Nothing could seem more discontinuous than the beginning of human life in a virgin womb. At the same time, the angel announces this breaking of the Word of God into her womb and into history in terms of its fulfillment of Jewish history, for he tells her that her son will sit on the throne of David and rule the house of Jacob (see Luke 1:31–33).

Why would God choose a girl from the unimportant town of Nazareth? At the same time that this is a surprise, it seems in accord with so many seemingly unlikely and mysterious choices throughout the Old Testament: Abraham, Sarah,

Moses, David, Elisha and so forth. Mary, however, is the pinnacle of God's method of preference, of choosing one person not to the exclusion of others but that others may be chosen. In her case the rest of us may become sons and daughters of God our Father as well as the sons and daughters of Mary.

It is said that every Jewish girl has secretly hoped to be the mother of the Messiah, and Mary was a Jewish girl, raised and educated by her people. As much as the Annunciation was a surprise, it also must have been somehow awaited. Mary faced utter surprise and utter correspondence at the same time. Her yes was not only the fruit of her sinlessness but also the fruit of her Jewishness. Her yes was full of her belonging to her people. It was the fruit of the familiarity that the chosen people had come to have with God. It was the fruit of a people who remained faithful to a God who keeps his promises in the most unpredictable ways.

Mary was a faithful Jew who, because of the history of her people, had come to expect God to do the unexpected. She had heard of so many before her who seemed unimportant and yet were called by God to pivotal roles in his plan of salvation. The proposal of the angel was surprising but not absurd. It would continue to be surprising, perhaps, because of how much sense it would actually make, a deeper sense than human reason could ever attain on its own.

Mary represents both a continuation of salvation history and at the same time an utterly new event. She is one with the women of the Old Testament who rejoice at their surprised fruitfulness. Her Magnificat (see Luke 1:46–55) echoes the thanksgiving prayer of Hannah, the mother of Samuel (1 Samuel 2:1–10).

Hannah had been barren, as had been Sarah and as was Elizabeth, Mary's cousin. God had taken pity on barren wombs of women who cried out to him. Mary belongs to this tradition of God's grace and at the same time bursts through that tradition with a previously inconceivable (or perhaps "unconceived") grace: Mary's was not a barren but a virgin womb, which grace filled with a Presence that none would have thought to ask for.

Jesus himself is the New Covenant, which means Mary is the new ark of the covenant. We have looked already at the woman in Revelation 12. Let us now look at what precedes the description of this woman at the end of Revelation 11 (understanding that this book, like all the others in the Bible, was not originally broken into separate chapters): "Then God's temple in heaven was opened, and the ark of his covenant was seen within his temple; and there were flashes of lightning, rumblings, peals of thunder, an earthquake, and heavy hail" (Revelation 11:19). Then Revelation 12 tells us: "A great portent appeared in heaven: a woman clothed with the sun…. She was pregnant" (12:1–2).

The woman with child is the ark of the covenant that the visionary sees in the temple. As the old ark carried the tablets of the Ten Commandments, Mary carries Jesus.

We also see Mary as the ark of the covenant in Luke's Gospel, when John the Baptist leaps for joy upon hearing the voice of Mary greet Elizabeth. John the Baptist leaps before Mary, the new ark of the covenant, as David danced for joy before the old ark when it was brought to him in Jerusalem (see 2 Samuel 6:14–15). In carrying Jesus, Mary carries her people from the old covenant to the new.

A MOTHERLY GUIDE TO SALVATION HISTORY

Salvation has a mother!

A good friend of mine was visiting her daughter and granddaughter one weekend. There was an awkwardness when Sunday morning came, because my friend is Catholic and her daughter left the Church for an evangelical church that is suspicious of Catholic teaching. As my friend was leaving for Mass, her four-year-old granddaughter begged to go with her. The young girl's mother begrudgingly allowed it.

After Mass, as grandmother and granddaughter were leaving the church, the girl noticed a statue in the middle of the lawn.

"What's that, Grandma?"

"It's a statue of Mary."

"Who's Mary?"

The shocked grandma responded, "The mother of Jesus!"

The equally shocked granddaughter replied, "Jesus had a mother?!"

In that moment, for that little girl, Jesus became human. Someone whom she had learned about as Lord had become like her in all things but sin. She could relate to him now as she never could before.

Our temptation is to turn Jesus into an abstract idea: the greatest idea I can have of the greatest and most loving and most wonderful person possible. The problem with that is that Jesus is not my idea, and the way he loves doesn't always fit with my idea of loving.

Recall that the resurrected Jesus did not fit the apostles' idea, even after Jesus had predicted his resurrection to them three times (see Mark 8:31; 9:31; 10:34). After Pentecost the apostles likely didn't fit the idea many people had of the continuation of Christ's presence on earth.

Mary is the one who corrects the temptation to "de-incarnate" Jesus, because Jesus had a mother! Isn't it interesting that Mary is present at Pentecost (see Acts 1:14; 2:1)? The Holy Spirit, who made Jesus a physical presence in Mary's womb, now makes Jesus physically present among the apostles. Mary must have recognized her Son in those spirit-filled apostles! Mary understands that the Holy Spirit is not abstract. He seeks to make Jesus present in ways we can see and touch.

Some ancient writers have speculated about how sad Mary must have been to have lived with John after Jesus ascended into heaven, but I wonder if this is true. For when we receive the Holy Spirit and are open to a community life and a sacramental life in the Church, we come to resemble Jesus. Mary must have marveled at how the Word was becoming flesh through John. With him she must have begun to ponder in her heart what it meant to be the Mother of the Church. For the flesh that grew in her womb was now beginning to grow throughout the world and throughout history.

Jesus is not an idea. The fruit of Mary's womb continues to live in the Church: in her members and in her sacraments.

MARY'S SINLESSNESS AND GOD'S LOVE

Mary is conceived without sin. If the seeds of this truth are found in Scripture and have flowered in the doctrine of the Church, there must be reason for us to know this. Let us consider how Mary's sinlessness can help us look more clearly at salvation history. We can discover that sin is not a mere breaking of rules and that God is not a mere instrument that I use to gain moral perfection.

Sin is there at the very beginning of human history, and sin is vanquished at the climactic moments of the cross and the Resurrection. Sin and mercy are present throughout the Old and New Testaments. Mercy, in fact, is one of the main ways that we recognize the promise of salvation through the presence of God.

However, if we don't understand the nature of sin, we can reduce salvation history to a legalistic "cleaning of the slate" so I can measure up and do better next time. The faith can decay into a moralistic view of God and his action in the world. We can think that God is somehow a means to our becoming better rule-followers.

I teach in an all boys' high school. I have daily empirical evidence that becoming good rule-followers is not an enticing goal for the human person.

Knowing of Mary's sinlessness helps us to understand the nature of sin and the nature of God's love as our destiny and fulfillment. Recall that the serpent told Eve that God did not want her to eat the forbidden fruit because "God knows that when you eat of it your eyes will be opened, and you will be like God, knowing good and evil" (Genesis 3:5). The temptation for Eve, then, is that if she takes the fruit, she will become like God. If she becomes like God, then she won't need God anymore. She will be her own god.

The serpent's temptation proposes a view of reality in which the goal is not union with God but an independent "godlike" state in which I don't need any relationship. How insidious! This is a temptation all of us can fall into with the best of intentions. I think I am going to be good all by myself and somehow impress God.

Mary corrects this lie of "holy independence." Mary has no sin, but no created person is as totally dependent on God as she is. She is full of grace, which is the life of God! Everything she is and does is a reflection of God's love, a flowering of her communion with the Father, Son and Holy Spirit.

The goal of life is not some abstract perfection but remaining in God's love. This love is not impersonal: Jesus gave it a face (thanks to Mary!) and revealed it to us as our Father. The goal is not alienated perfection but perpetual communion.

Mary shows the serpent's proposal to be the lie that it is. For my freedom from sin does not give me independence from God; this idea is exactly the opposite of the truth. The less sin I have, the more I am in relationship with God!

Sin is alienation from this relationship that generates me. Hell is a state in which I am lost in myself; and this is exactly where the serpent's proposed view of reality leads. The freer I am from sin, the more I experience myself as a beloved son or daughter, and the more I understand that the goal of my life is neither rule-following nor self-perfection. The goal of my life is the Father.

God was and is and ever shall be—Father, Son and Holy Spirit. To be like God is to be in communion, to perpetually receive and return and radiate this dynamic love. Mary proclaims and personifies the fact that our human fulfillment is to be in relationship with God: She is the daughter of the Father, the mother of the Son, the spouse of the Holy Spirit.

BORN OF ISRAEL, BORN OF WOMAN

"But when the fullness of time had come, God sent his Son, born of a woman, born under the law, in order to redeem those who were under the law, so that we might receive adoption as children" (Galatians 4:4–5).

"God is love" (1 John 4:8). Love is not abstract because God is not abstract. God didn't reveal himself merely spiritually; he chose a people. We can say that his presence first became tangible through this people.

You cannot have Jesus without the whole human history of the Jewish people, his people. If I love Jesus, then I have a profound respect and awe for the Jewish people. That woman in Revelation 12 is also a symbol for Israel, for it was from that nation's history, from its flesh, that Jesus came.

Jesus became flesh. He was a particular man who lived in a particular time and place and culture because Mary said yes. It was from her flesh that Jesus came. I cannot love Jesus without loving his mother as my mother, for he gave her to me. He deliberately gave her to all of us at the cross, that most profound expression of God's love (see John 19:27).

Whenever Blessed Teresa of Calcutta was asked why Catholics honor Mary, her response would be, "No Mary, no Jesus." I will extend this simple response in order to extend our respect and gratitude to the Jewish people: "No Israel, no Mary; no Mary, no Jesus; no Israel, no people to whom Jesus can begin to reveal God, who is love."

We can conclude this reflection with a cue from a prayer of the Church, the Divine Praises:

Blessed be God.
Blessed be his holy name.

Blessed be Jesus Christ, true God and true man....
Blessed be the Holy Spirit, the Paraclete.
Blessed be the great Mother of God, Mary most holy.
Blessed be God in his chosen people, the family of Mary, the forebears of Christ.
Blessed be God in his holy Church, the children of Mary, the body of Christ.[2]

FOR REFLECTION:

1. Do I tend to reduce Christianity to moral regulations?

2. Am I joyful because of my awareness of the presence and the reality of Jesus Christ?

3. Can I find in my own experience the desire for union with God the Father? Do I recognize in myself an infinite need for a father—for the Father?

Notes

Foreword

1. Joseph Ratzinger, *Salt of the Earth: The Church at the End of the Millennium* (San Francisco: Ignatius, 1997), pp. 247, 248.

2. The quote in *CCC* 122 is from the Second Vatican Council, *Dei Verbum*, Dogmatic Constitution on Divine Revelation, 19.

Introduction: The Long-Awaited Messiah, the Promised of Ages

1. Luigi Giussani, *The Psalms*, William Vouk, trans. (New York: Crossroad, 2004), p. 9.

Chapter One: What Makes the Chosen People Unique?

1. Thomas Cahill, *The Gifts of the Jews: How a Tribe of Desert Nomads Changed the Way Everyone Thinks and Feels* (New York: Doubleday, 1998) p. 5.

Chapter Two: God and Man: Two Creation Stories

1. See Pope Pius XII, *Humani Generis,* Encyclical Concerning Some False Opinions Threatening to Undermine the Foundations of Catholic Doctrine, nos. 37–39, at www.vatican.va.

2. Vatican Council II, *Gaudium et Spes*, Pastoral Constitution on the Church in the Modern World, December 7, 1965, no. 22, in Austin P. Flannery, ed., *Documents of Vatican II* (Grand Rapids, Mich.: Eerdmans, 1978), p. 922, quoted by Pope John Paul II in *Redemptor Hominis*, Encyclical on the Redeemer of Man, March 4, 1979, no. 8.

3. *Order of Christian Funerals* (New York: Catholic Book Publishing Co., 1989), p. 31. Translation copyright: ICEL, 1985.

Chapter Three: Adam and Eve and Jesus and Mary

1. See Pope Pius XII, nos. 37–38.

Chapter Six: Mystery Men of Old and New

1. Eucharistic Prayer I, *The Roman Missal* (Washington: ICEL, 1973).

2. Luigi Giussani, *Why the Church?* Vivianne Hewitt, trans. (Montreal: McGill-Queen's University Press, 2000), pp. 119–120.

Chapter Seven: Joseph and Jesus

1. Luigi Giussani, *Tu (O dell' amicizia)* (Milan: Biblioteca Universali Rizzoli, 1997), vol. 1, p. 239.

2. From the Exultet, Liturgy of the Easter Vigil. See *Catechism of the Catholic Church*, no. 412.

Chapter Eleven: Elijah and Elisha and the Ascension

1. Eucharistic Prayer I.

2. Giussani, *Why the Church?* p. 131.

Chapter Twelve: Mary of Israel: Through Her the Old Is Made New

1. Pope Benedict XVI, *Deus Caritas Est*, Encyclical Letter on Christian Love, December 25, 2005, par. 1. Luigi Giussani, *The Risk of Education: Discovering Our Ultimate Destiny*, Rosanna M. Giammanco Frongia, trans. (New York: Crossroad, 2001), p. 25. Pope John Paul II, *Angelus*, September 15, 1996, par. 2, www.ewtn.com.

2. Excerpt from "The Divine Praises," as found in *St. Joseph Weekday Missal*, vol. 2 (New York: Catholic Book, 1975), p. 1282.

Bibliography

Boadt, Lawrence. *Reading the Old Testament: An Introduction.* New York: Paulist, 1984.

Bright, John. *A History of Ancient Israel,* third edition. Philadelphia: Westminster, 1981.

Cahill, Thomas. *The Gifts of the Jews: How a Tribe of Desert Nomads Changed the Way Everyone Thinks and Feels.* New York: Doubleday, 1998.

Giussani, Luigi. *At the Origin of the Christian Claim.* Vivianne Hewitt, trans. Montreal: McGill-Queen's University Press, 1998.

———. *The Psalms.* William Vouk III, trans. New York: Crossroads, 2004.

———. *The Religious Sense.* John Zucchi, trans. Montreal: McGill-Queen's University Press, 1997.

———. *The Risk of Education: Discovering Our Ultimate Destiny.* Rosanna M. Giammanco Frongia, trans. New York: Crossroad, 2001.

———. *Why the Church?* Vivianne Hewitt, trans. Montreal: McGill-Queen's University Press, 2001.

Hahn, Scott. *Hail Holy Queen: The Mother of God in the Word of God.* New York: Doubleday, 2001.

Pope Benedict XVI. *Deus Caritas Est*, Encyclical Letter on Christian Love. December 25, 2005. www.vatican.va.

Pope John Paul II. *Redemptor Hominis*, Encyclical Letter on Redemption and the Dignity of the Human Race. March 4, 1979. www.vatican.va.

Pope Pius XII. *Humani Generis*, Encyclical Letter Concerning Some False Opinions Threatening to Undermine the Foundations of Catholic Doctrine. August 12, 1950. www.vatican.va.

Vatican Council II. *Gaudium et Spes*, Pastoral Constitution on the Church in the Modern World. December 7, 1965. In Austin P. Flannery, ed. *Documents of Vatican II* (Grand Rapids, Mich.: Eerdmans, 1978), pp. 903–1014.